DESSERTS
FOR EVERY MOOD

First published in hardback India by
HarperCollins *Publishers* 2020
Building No 10, Tower A, 4th Floor, DLF Cyber City, Phase II,
Gurugram – 122002
www.harpercollins.co.in

This edition published by
HarperCollins *Publishers* 2024

2 4 6 8 10 9 7 5 3 1

P-ISBN: 9789365697322
E-ISBN: 9789353577346

Book design: Bonita Vaz-Shimray, Isha Nagar, Sanjeev Kumar
Cover and section opener photographs: Saumya Gupta

Printed and bound at
Replika Press Pvt. Ltd.

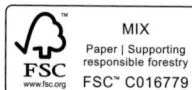

MIX
Paper | Supporting
responsible forestry
FSC
www.fsc.org
FSC™ C016779

SHIVESH BHATIA'S

DESSERTS
FOR EVERY MOOD
100 *feel-good recipes*

HarperCollins *Publishers* India

CONVERSION TABLE

PRODUCT	1 CUP	½ CUP	¼ CUP
FLOUR	120g	60g	30g
BUTTER	220g	110g	55g
CASTER SUGAR	220g	110g	55g
BROWN SUGAR	200g	100g	50g
ICING SUGAR	120g	60g	30g
LIQUID	200g	100g	50g

1 Tablespoon: 15g   1 Teaspoon: 5g

A note on the ingredients
Unless otherwise mentioned, for best results,
use ingredients at room temperature.
All recipes in this book use salted
butter, that is softened, unless specified.
For recipes that require Greek yogurt,
you can also use hung curd.

CONTENTS

INTRODUCTION

When I first started baking, as a young sixteen-year-old boy, it was something that allowed me to disconnect with the world after a stressful day at college and find some time for myself. I remember how I used to go to the kitchen, past midnight, and quietly gather all the ingredients so I wouldn't wake my parents up with all the noise.

Back then, more often than not, the desserts I baked weren't as elaborate or fancy – sometimes, they weren't even that great! But the process of creating those desserts from scratch kept me glued to the kitchen. As I baked, I'd forget about everything around – my phone, the fact that I'd been on my feet for hours at length, or that I had to be in college at 8 a.m. the next day. Baking helped me focus on the present and really immerse myself in the process of whipping up something sweet and delicious.

I didn't bake every day then. I would only enter the kitchen when I really felt like picking up the whisk, when I wanted to bake something for my family and friends, or when I needed something to help take my mind off unpleasant thoughts. But this changed after a few months, and somewhere I lost touch with the process, which I realized only later.

When I began blogging full-time in 2017, baking became a part of my job. I am not complaining – I was grateful to be able to combine my passion and career, but somewhere the focus shifted. Now, I was baking every day, not for myself but to share recipes on the website and images on my social media. While I truly enjoyed every second of my work, I realized baking had become something completely different from what it had meant seven years ago. In time, as my professional journey continued, I came to have a stunning studio kitchen, and now I bake there almost every day with my team, and together we create content that has allowed me to connect with people across the world. I treasure that warm connection with people, but last year I decided to re-establish my relationship with baking, and as a consequence reconnect with myself too.

After I sent in my recipes for the first book in 2018, I felt I wasn't doing enough. To fill that void, I decided to enrol myself into a postgraduate course. After clearing a written entrance exam, a group discussion round and an interview, I found myself in a classroom studying advertising and public relations at one of the most prestigious colleges in the country. But after two months, I realized I had gotten myself into something I did not enjoy. I woke up every morning not wanting to get out of bed. I did not enjoy being in the classroom and came back physically and mentally exhausted, with no time and energy to work on my blog. While the course was definitely not my cup of tea, my time in college taught me two very important things.

For starters, it made me realize the value of the work I had been doing for the past few years and how deeply I enjoyed doing it. They say you realize the importance of something once it's taken away from you and that is exactly what happened. Those seven hours of attending classes in college, two hours of commute and a few more hours spent on completing assignments left me with no time to do what I love – to create content, share my recipes, style and photograph my desserts and travel. I remember giving an interview to *The Hindu* during this time. The reporter asked me how my experience of blogging full-time for a year was and I clearly remember saying, 'It was the best year of my life. I'll be a happy boy if the rest of my life would be like that one year.'

That is when it hit me, I was trying to fix something that wasn't broken – that one year of my life *could* be the rest of life.

Those two months of being away from my work made me grateful for the opportunities I had, my team and for the freedom of being able to follow my passion. Two months later, I made the decision to drop out of college and focus on my blog again. It wasn't an easy decision at all and for the first time I was plagued by doubt. I had joined college seeing my friends and everyone around me trying to bag that next degree. But now, even though I would be working, I was worried dropping out would make things worse.

But as it turned out, in retrospect, dropping out was the best decision of my life. I woke up with a different kind of energy, raring to go and excited to create new and interesting recipes and photos.

But this time, there was a difference. Even though I knew I was immersing myself into content creation like before, I also knew that I wanted to take out time to bake for myself. After a long day of baking, styling desserts, photographing them, uploading recipes and pictures, I would find myself in the kitchen every night, all by myself, baking a batch of warm, gooey brownies. Chopping up a slab of dark chocolate into chunks, melting it with butter into a smooth, sumptuous-smelling mixture gave me happiness that I cannot put into words.

Since then, I have started paying more attention to the process of baking and to the small details that go into it. For someone like me who bakes so many desserts day in and day out, it is inevitable that one starts working on autopilot, but this time I decided to slow down. I paused and took time to understand the ingredients I was working with. I wanted to experience everything, like the sensation of kneading the dough with my fingers. I enjoyed the fresh fragrance of lime zest as I prepped it for a cake. I would sit and watch my eclairs puff up, all golden, in the oven. Now, instead of jumping from one recipe to another, I would station myself in front of the oven and watch my desserts

magically transform. I now give myself time and space – before I even begin a recipe, I take a moment to picture my dessert, and patiently and carefully measure all the ingredients, slowly letting the recipe choreograph my thoughts and emotions.

There are days when I find myself completely uninspired. On some days, I feel the pressure of churning out new content. Sometimes, a hateful comment will upset me. While on other days I might be sad because I have fought with a friend. On these days, baking becomes my saviour. It becomes my creative expression, it stimulates my senses and engages more than just my taste buds. I have always said that what fascinates me the most about baking is how simple ingredients like flour, sugar, eggs, butter, transform in the oven into fluffy goodness. But move beyond the mechanical measuring, pouring and stirring, and you get something that pushes away all the stress and anxiety.

It's magical, what baking does to your senses. When you pause to experience the process of baking, each sense gets heightened and you can't help but be grateful. To be able to smell the hazelnuts getting roasted. To see white sugar turn into beautiful amber caramel. To feel the softness of the butter turn between my fingers when I'm making my pie dough. To taste the pleasant contrast of sea salt against the sweetness of cocoa in my favourite chocolate chunk cookies. To hear the whisk click against the bowl as I cream the sugar and butter together. Taking it slow and immersing myself in the experience, carrying out every step mindfully has made me feel closer to the desserts I bake.

The life-affirming journey that baking takes you on is something I was reminded of by someone else, too, recently. One of my readers confided in me about a terrible experience she went through in the tenth grade. In a miserable state of mind, and buckling under the immense academic pressure, she decided to try out recipes from my blog. In her message to me, she said my recipes helped her at the lowest point in her life and gave her purpose. This is the magic and power of baking – it takes up

all your attention and makes you focus on the task at hand, breaking negative thought patterns and makes you feel in command of your ideas and emotions.

In this book, I am putting together 100 recipes that I have absolutely enjoyed creating in my kitchen. Some recipes are very simple and you'd be able to whip them up in no time, others are slightly more complex. I promise the end result of each recipe will make you and others around you very happy, but it is up to you to also enjoy the process. Whatever you decide to bake from this book, don't forget to give each recipe the time and space it deserves. Go through the recipe carefully, visualize it. Gather your ingredients and immerse yourself in the process of whipping up that delicious dessert. Enjoy the colours, textures, smells, touch and the taste. Let baking soothe all your stresses and woes and let the immense sense of peace and calm wash over you as your kitchen fills up with the fragrance of warmth and love.

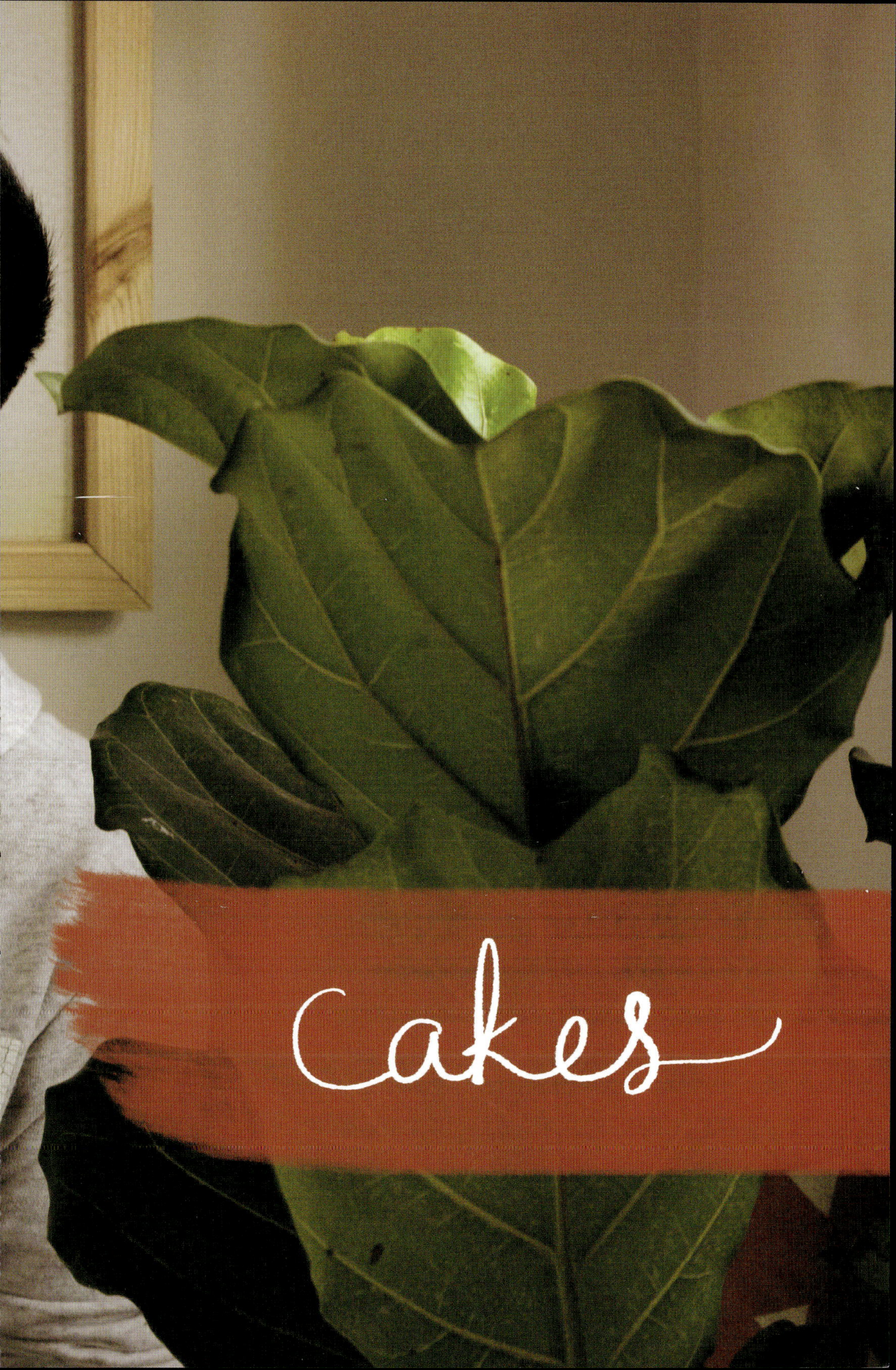

Cakes

PEACH AND BLUEBERRY CAKE

This peach and blueberry cake recipe is one of my favourites because I love baking with Greek yogurt. This cake has an incredible texture and a delightful mix of flavours from the lemon, peaches and blueberries. You won't be able to stop yourself from devouring it down to its last crumb!

INGREDIENTS

¾ cup all-purpose flour

2 teaspoons baking powder

1 teaspoon lemon zest

¾ cup light brown sugar

⅔ cup vegetable oil

1 cup Greek yogurt

2 teaspoons vanilla extract

¼ cup milk

4–5 peaches, sliced

¼ cup blueberries

METHOD

1. Preheat the oven to 180°C. Line an 8-inch round cake pan with parchment paper.

2. In a bowl, combine the flour, baking powder and lemon zest.

3. In another bowl, beat the sugar and oil for about 3–4 minutes. Mix in the yogurt and the vanilla extract. Slowly beat the milk into this mixture.

4. Fold the dry ingredients into the wet ingredients, mixing until everything is combined. Do not overmix.

5. Transfer the batter into the prepared pan and arrange the peach slices and blueberries over it.

6. Bake for 35–40 minutes or until a skewer inserted into the centre of the cake comes out clean.

CHOCOLATE ESPRESSO CARAMEL CAKE

I made this chocolate Bundt cake with espresso caramel as an impromptu dessert and it turned out to be so delicious and elegant, I just had to share it with you!

INGREDIENTS

For the cake

1½ cups all-purpose flour

¾ cup cocoa powder

2 teaspoons espresso powder

½ teaspoon baking soda

1 teaspoon baking powder

¾ cup butter

1¼ cups caster sugar

2 eggs

½ cup milk

For the espresso caramel

1 cup granulated sugar

½ cup butter

½ cup warm cream

1 shot brewed espresso

1 cup chopped mixed nuts

METHOD

1. Preheat the oven to 180°C. Grease a 9-inch Bundt pan, or an 8-inch round cake tin with parchment paper.

2. In a bowl, whisk the flour, cocoa powder, espresso powder, baking soda and baking powder, and set aside.

3. In another bowl, beat the butter and sugar until the mixture is light and fluffy. Add the eggs and mix well.

4. Fold the dry ingredients into the wet ingredients in three batches, beginning and ending with the flour mixture, and alternating with the milk. Mix until just combined. Do not overmix.

5. Pour the batter into the prepared cake pan and bake for 30–40 minutes, or until a toothpick inserted in the centre comes out clean. Let the cake cool, then carefully unmould it.

6. To make the caramel, heat the sugar in a saucepan over medium heat until it turns amber in colour. Whisk in the butter until it has completely melted. Add the warm cream, whisking constantly as the mixture will bubble up vigorously.

7. Transfer the caramel to a clean bowl, and add the shot of espresso and fold in the mixed nuts.

8. Pour the caramel mixture, while it is still runny, but not very hot, over the cake.

STRAWBERRY ALMOND CAKE

All my readers seem to love desserts that have almonds and fruit in them. This recipe is inspired by one of the most popular desserts on my blog: the orange almond cake.

INGREDIENTS

1½ cups all-purpose flour
¾ cup ground almonds
(ground with the skin on)
2 teaspoons baking powder
1 teaspoon baking soda
½ cup butter
1 cup caster sugar
4 eggs (or 2 cups
Greek yogurt)
1 teaspoon vanilla extract or
2 drops almond essence
1 cup chopped fresh
strawberries
Flaked almonds, to top

METHOD

1. Preheat the oven to 180°C. Line an 8-inch round cake pan with parchment paper.

2. In a bowl, whisk together the flour, ground almonds, baking powder and baking soda.

3. In another bowl, beat the butter and sugar until light and creamy. Add the eggs, one at a time (or yogurt, if using), beating well after each addition. Add the vanilla extract (or almond essence, if using).

4. Fold the dry ingredients into the wet ingredients, mixing until everything is combined. Do not overmix. Gently fold in the fresh strawberries, reserving some for the top.

5. Transfer the batter into the prepared pan. Top with flaked almonds and the remaining strawberries.

6. Bake for 30–35 minutes, or until a skewer inserted into the centre of the cake comes out clean.

THREE-LAYER VANILLA CAKE

Whether you're hosting an elegant dinner party or simply want to finish your weekend family lunch with an easy dessert, this layered vanilla cake with blueberry compote is sure to hit the sweet spot!

INGREDIENTS

For the cake

3 cups all-purpose flour
3 teaspoons baking powder
¾ teaspoon baking soda
¾ cup vegetable oil
1½ cups caster sugar
2 teaspoons pure vanilla extract
1½ cups Greek yogurt
½ cup milk

For the topping

3 cups blueberry compote (see p. 151)
2 cups cream cheese frosting (see p. 139)
Fresh blueberries and edible flowers

METHOD

1. Preheat oven to 180°C. Line three 6-inch round pans with parchment paper.

2. In a bowl, sift together the flour, baking powder and baking soda.

3. In another bowl, beat together the oil and sugar until the mixture is pale and light. Beat in the vanilla extract and yogurt.

4. Gently fold the dry ingredients into the wet ingredients in two batches, alternating with the milk. Mix until everything is just combined and no large flour pockets are visible. Do not overmix.

5. Divide the batter equally between the prepared cake pans. Bake for 30–35 minutes or until a skewer inserted in the centre of the cake comes out clean.

6. Allow the cakes to cool on a wire rack completely before frosting.

7. Generously top a layer of cake with a dollop of cream cheese frosting and spread some blueberry compote over it. Place another cake layer on top of it and repeat the process until all the layers are done. Decorate with fresh blueberries and edible flowers.

GRAPEFRUIT MADELEINES

Light, fluffy and delicious, madeleines are a French classic. Traditionally, they are decorated with coconut and jam but we're taking things to a new level by infusing grapefruit in these soft cakes.

INGREDIENTS

½ cup butter

1 tablespoon grapefruit juice

6 tablespoons milk

1 bag Earl Grey tea

1 cup all-purpose flour

½ teaspoon baking powder

1 tablespoon grapefruit zest

1 tablespoon flax
seed powder

2 tablespoons water

½ cup caster sugar

1 teaspoon vanilla extract

METHOD

1. Preheat the oven to 180°C. Lightly grease a madeleine mould with butter.

2. Melt the butter in a saucepan set over medium heat. Turn off the heat and add the grapefruit juice. Set aside.

3. In another saucepan, heat the milk until just warm, then add a bag of Earl Grey tea and let it infuse for 4-5 minutes. Take it off the heat and let it cool.

4. In a bowl, whisk together the flour, baking powder and grapefruit zest, and set aside.

5. In another bowl, mix the flax seed powder with water and let the mixture stand for 5 minutes. Add the sugar to the flax seed mixture and beat until pale and fluffy.

6. Gently fold the flour mixture into the flax seed mixture using a spatula. Add the melted butter and vanilla extract, and mix until combined. Add the Earl Grey-infused milk. Mix well.

7. Transfer the batter into a piping bag and pipe it into the prepared madeleine pan.

8. Bake for 12–15 minutes, or until the madeleines turn golden brown.

CHOCOLATE MANGO CAKE

This recipe brings together two of my favourite flavours and if you had any doubts about the combination of mango and chocolate, you won't have them once you try this cake – because this is D.E.L.I.C.I.O.U.S.

INGREDIENTS

For the cake

3 cups all-purpose flour

1½ cups cocoa powder

2 teaspoons baking powder

1 teaspoon baking soda

1½ cups vegetable oil

3 cups caster sugar

2 cups Greek yogurt

1 cup milk

For the topping

3 cups chocolate cream cheese frosting (see p. 148)

3 mangoes, peeled and sliced

METHOD

1. Preheat the oven to 180°C. Line four 6-inch baking pans with parchment paper.

2. Sift together the flour, cocoa powder, baking powder and baking soda into a bowl.

3. In a large bowl, beat the oil and sugar with an electric mixer until the mixture is pale. Add the yogurt to the oil mixture and mix well. Add the milk.

4. Carefully fold the dry ingredients into the wet ingredients until no large flour pockets are visible. Do not overmix.

5. Distribute the batter equally into the four cake pans. Bake for 30 minutes, or until a skewer inserted in the centre of the cake comes out clean.

6. Allow the cakes to cool on a wire rack completely before frosting.

7. Generously top one layer of chocolate cake with the chocolate cream cheese frosting. Place another cake layer on top of it and repeat the process until all the layers are done. Remember to frost the outside of the cake as well.

8. Carefully place the slices of mango on top of the cake outside-in to form a flower-like arrangement.

APPLE HAZELNUT CAKE

I've always paired apples with almonds for my desserts, but with this cake I discovered how beautifully apples go with hazelnuts. Imagine having this cake with a cup of coffee on a chilly evening. And the best part: it's gluten free!

INGREDIENTS

For the hazelnut streusel

⅓ cup butter, softened
⅓ cup brown sugar
1 cup ground hazelnuts
¼ cup hazelnuts, chopped

For the cake

1 cup tapioca flour
1 cup ground hazelnuts
2 teaspoons baking powder
½ teaspoon cinnamon powder
¼ teaspoon ginger powder
½ cup olive oil
1 cup light brown sugar
4 eggs
¼ cup milk
2 apples, sliced

For the topping

Lemon Curd (see p. 156)
Cream Cheese Frosting
(see p. 139)

METHOD

1. To make the hazelnut streusel, combine the butter, brown sugar, ground hazelnuts and chopped hazelnuts in a bowl. It should have a crumb-like texture. Refrigerate for 30 minutes.

2. Preheat the oven to 180°C. Line an 8-inch round cake pan with parchment paper.

3. In a bowl, combine the tapioca flour, ground hazelnuts, baking powder, cinnamon and ginger powders, and set aside.

4. In another bowl, beat the oil and sugar together. Beat in the eggs, one at a time, mixing well after each addition.

5. Fold the dry ingredients into the wet ingredients using a spatula. Now add the milk, and mix well.

6. Pour the batter into the prepared cake pan and arrange the apple slices on top. Scatter the chilled streusel crumbs over the apples and cake batter.

7. Bake for 25–30 minutes, or until a skewer inserted in the centre of the cake comes out clean.

8. Once the cake has cooled, you can pipe lemon curd and cream cheese frosting on top to make it even better!

STRAWBERRY SWISS ROLL

This is my version of a classic Swiss roll. A soft, airy vanilla sponge with a delicious sweet–tart strawberry filling, this is totally worth the patience and effort needed to make it.

INGREDIENTS

For the cake

⅓ cup all-purpose flour

3 tablespoons cornflour

5 eggs

½ cup plus 2 tablespoons caster sugar

1 teaspoon vanilla extract

Confectioners' sugar, for dusting

For the filling

1 cup heavy cream

½ teaspoon vanilla extract

4 tablespoons caster sugar

2 cups chopped strawberries

For the topping

Whipped cream

Fresh fruit

METHOD

1. Preheat the oven to 230°C. Butter a 17x12-inch baking pan, line it with parchment paper, and then butter and flour the paper.

2. To make the cake, sift the flour and cornflour into a bowl, and set aside.

3. Separate two eggs, and set aside the egg whites in a clean dry bowl. In another bowl, beat the two egg yolks, the three whole eggs and ½ cup sugar on high speed until pale and fluffy. Add the vanilla extract.

4. Fold the sifted flour into the egg mixture in two batches. Mix until just combined.

5. Beat the egg whites until foamy. Add 2 tablespoons of sugar and continue beating until the egg whites form stiff peaks. Gently fold the egg whites into the flour and egg mixture in three batches. Do not overmix or you will knock out all the air. Transfer the batter into the prepared baking pan and spread evenly.

6. Bake for about 6–8 minutes or until golden brown. Remove the cake from the oven and immediately sprinkle confectioners' sugar over it. Invert the cake onto a clean dish towel, remove the parchment paper, and sprinkle confectioners' sugar. Roll up the sponge with the towel. Place on a wire rack to cool.

7. To make the filling, whip the cream, vanilla extract and sugar into the bowl. Beat until soft peaks form. Add the strawberry.

8. Unroll the sponge. Spread with the filling and reroll the cake. Cover and chill in the refrigerator for a few hours. Just before serving, dust with confectioners' sugar and decorate with whipped cream.

ORANGE CAKE

This light, fluffy and zesty eggless orange cake is the perfect partner for your evening cup of tea!

INGREDIENTS

For the cake

1½ cups all-purpose flour

1 teaspoon baking powder

1 cup Greek yogurt

½ teaspoon baking soda

¾ cup caster sugar

½ cup vegetable oil

Zest of 1 orange

¼ cup orange juice

1 teaspoon vanilla extract

For the topping

1 cup vanilla buttercream
(see p. 155)

1 orange, sliced

¼ cup blueberries

METHOD

1. Preheat the oven to 180°C. Line an 8-inch round cake pan with parchment paper.

2. In a bowl, whisk together the flour and baking powder, and set aside.

3. Take the yogurt in a small bowl and mix in the baking soda. Set aside for 5–6 minutes for it to foam up.

4. In another bowl, whisk together the sugar, oil, orange zest and orange juice until pale. Add the yogurt to the oil and sugar mixture, and mix well. Add the vanilla extract.

5. Gently fold the dry ingredients into the wet ingredients, mixing until everything is combined and no large flour pockets are visible. Do not overmix.

6. Pour the batter into the prepared cake pan. Bake for 30–35 minutes, or until a skewer inserted in the centre of the cake comes out clean.

7. Cool the cake on a wire rack.

8. Top the cooled cake with vanilla buttercream and decorate with orange slices and blueberries.

LEMON SHEET CAKE

Lemon is an incredibly versatile ingredient and it effortlessly contributes so much to a dessert. This cake is flavoured using both lemon zest and lemon juice, and topped with a smooth vanilla buttercream frosting. If you love lemon in your desserts, make these lemon cake squares right away!

INGREDIENTS

For the cake

1½ cups all-purpose flour
1 teaspoon baking powder
½ teaspoon baking soda
1 tablespoon lemon zest
¾ cup vegetable oil
1½ cups caster sugar
1 cup Greek yogurt
½ teaspoon vanilla extract
5 tablespoons lemon juice
½ cup milk mixed with 1 teaspoon lemon juice, rested for 5 minutes

For the topping

1 cup vanilla buttercream frosting (see p. 155)
½ cup freeze-dried raspberries, crushed

METHOD

1. Preheat the oven to 180°C. Line an 8-inch square pan with parchment paper.

2. In a large bowl, combine the flour, baking powder, baking soda and lemon zest. Set aside.

3. In another bowl, beat the oil and sugar until the mixture is pale. Beat in the yogurt, vanilla extract and lemon juice.

4. Fold the dry ingredients into the wet ingredients in three batches, starting and ending with the flour mixture and alternating with the milk. Do not overmix.

5. Transfer the batter into the prepared cake pan. Bake for 35–40 minutes, or until a skewer inserted in the centre of the cake comes out clean.

6. Allow the cake to cool on a wire rack.

7. Generously cover the cooled cake with buttercream frosting and the crushed raspberries. Cut it into squares.

PINEAPPLE UPSIDE-DOWN CAKE

This cake is a classic! Tender, juicy slices of pineapple on a basic white sponge – you cannot go wrong with this cake. The simplicity of the recipe makes me go back to it time and again.

INGREDIENTS

For the topping

1 tablespoon butter
5–6 tablespoons brown sugar
6–7 pineapple slices

For the cake

2 cups all-purpose flour
4 teaspoons baking powder
½ cup vegetable oil
¾ cup caster sugar
1 cup Greek yogurt
¾ cup milk

METHOD

1. Preheat the oven to 180°C. Grease a 9-inch cake pan with butter and sprinkle the brown sugar evenly on the base. Arrange the pineapple slices in a neat layer on top of the sugar.

2. In a medium-sized bowl, whisk together the flour and baking powder.

3. In a large bowl, using an electric mixer, beat the oil and sugar until pale and light. With the mixer on low, whisk in the yogurt.

4. Add the dry ingredients to the wet ingredients, starting and ending with the dry ingredients and alternating with the milk. Beat until smooth. Do not overmix.

5. Carefully pour the batter over the arranged fruit and bake for 30–40 minutes until the top is golden-brown.

6. Let the cake rest in the pan for 10–15 minutes before turning it out.

WHITE FOREST CAKE

This cake is my spin on the classic black forest cake. This vanilla sponge layered with rich, creamy, whipped white chocolate ganache and fresh cherries will not let you down.

INGREDIENTS

For the cake

2½ cups all-purpose flour

2 teaspoons baking powder

½ cup butter

1½ cups caster sugar

3 eggs

1 teaspoon vanilla extract

1½ cups milk

1 cup pitted cherries

For the frosting

2 cups white chocolate, roughly chopped

2 cups fresh cream

1 cup sweetened heavy cream, whipped to stiff peaks

For the topping

Fresh cherries

White chocolate shavings

METHOD

1. Preheat the oven to 180°C. Line three 4-inch cake pans with parchment paper.

2. In a bowl, combine the all-purpose flour and baking powder, and set aside.

3. In another bowl, beat together the butter and sugar until light and fluffy. Add the eggs one at a time, beating well after each addition. Add the vanilla extract.

4. Fold the dry ingredients into the wet ingredients, beginning and ending with the flour mixture, and alternating with the milk. Mix until combined. Do not overmix. Gently fold in the pitted cherries.

5. Divide the batter between the prepared pans. Bake the layers for 25–30 minutes, or until a skewer inserted into the centre of the cakes comes out clean. Let the cakes cool on a wire rack.

6. For the frosting, place the chopped chocolate in a bowl. Take the fresh cream in a saucepan over medium heat and bring it to a simmer. Pour the hot cream over the chopped chocolate and let it rest for 5 minutes. Whisk the chocolate and cream mixture until combined, then place it in the fridge for about 30 minutes. Fold the cooled white chocolate ganache into the whipped cream until combined and smooth.

7. Generously top one layer of cake with the white chocolate frosting. Place another cake layer on top of it and repeat the process until all the layers are done. Remember to frost the outside of the cake as well. Decorate the cake with fresh cherries and white chocolate shavings.

CHOCOLATE MUD CAKE

Moist, decadent and so delicious, this cake is what every chocolate lover's dreams are made of! You can find me, spoon in hand, in front of the oven door even before the cake is done baking!

INGREDIENTS

1¾ cups all-purpose flour

2 teaspoons baking powder

1¼ cups butter

1 cup dark chocolate, coarsely chopped

1⅓ cups milk

1½ cups caster sugar

1 teaspoon vanilla extract

¼ cup cocoa powder

1 cup Greek yogurt

METHOD

1. Preheat the oven to 180°C. Prepare a 9-inch round cake pan.

2. In a bowl, sift together the flour and baking powder. Set aside.

3. In a saucepan, heat the butter, dark chocolate and milk, stirring with a whisk until everything is combined. Add the sugar, vanilla extract and cocoa powder. Mix well till you get a thick dark chocolate sauce. Once the sauce begins to simmer, take the saucepan off the heat. Let the mixture cool down completely, about 10–15 minutes.

4. Mix the yogurt into the cooled sauce.

5. Gently fold the dry ingredients into the wet ingredients.

6. Pour the batter into the prepared cake pan and bake for 30 minutes, or until a skewer inserted in the centre of the cake comes out clean.

7. Serve the cake while it's still warm.

MINI LEMON CHIFFON CAKES

I love chiffon cakes! The addition of lemon in this recipe gives the perfect zing to these light and airy confections.

INGREDIENTS

For the cake

4 eggs, separated
¾ cup caster sugar, divided
1 cup all-purpose flour
1 teaspoon baking powder
½ teaspoon baking soda
½ teaspoon salt
1 tablespoon lemon zest
¼ cup fresh lemon juice
¼ cup vegetable oil

For the topping

1 cup meringue frosting
(see p. 144)

METHOD

1. Preheat the oven to 170°C. Generously grease a 6-cupcake pan with oil.

2. In a bowl, using an electric mixer, beat the egg whites on high speed until they become foamy. While the mixer is still running, gradually add ¼ cup sugar. Keep beating until the egg whites form stiff peaks.

3. In another bowl, combine ½ cup sugar, flour, baking powder, baking soda, salt and lemon zest. Make a well in the dry ingredients and add the egg yolks, lemon juice and vegetable oil. Mix with a spatula until everything is combined.

4. Gently fold the whipped egg whites into the mixture in batches. Be careful not to mix vigorously and knock out the air.

5. Transfer the batter into the prepared pan and bake for 20–25 minutes, or until a skewer inserted into the centre comes out clean.

6. Once the cakes have cooled, pipe the meringue frosting on top and toast it using a kitchen torch.

BLACKBERRY AND FIG CAKE

I love baking with berries; they're like jewels for my desserts. When I got my hands on fresh blackberries and figs, I knew I had to bake something delicious! Every bite of this cake comes with a burst of flavour!

INGREDIENTS

3 cups all-purpose flour

3 teaspoons baking powder

¼ teaspoon salt

1 cup vegetable oil

1½ cups caster sugar

2 teaspoons vanilla extract

3 eggs

½ cup milk

1 cup fresh figs, sliced

1 cup fresh blackberries

METHOD

1. Preheat the oven to 180°C. Line an 8-inch round cake pan with parchment paper.

2. In a bowl, whisk together the flour, baking powder and salt, and set aside.

3. In another bowl, beat the oil and sugar together. Add the vanilla extract. Add the eggs, one at a time, mixing well after each addition. Whisk in the milk.

4. Gently fold the dry ingredients into the wet ingredients using a spatula. Mix until just combined. Do not overmix.

5. Pour the batter into the prepared cake pan and top it with figs and blackberries. Bake for 40–45 minutes, or until a skewer inserted into the centre of the cake comes out clean.

CHOCOLATE CAKE WITH SALTED CARAMEL GANACHE

I experiment with so many ingredients while coming up with recipes, and jowar flour has been one of the best surprises. This cake is SO good – it's super rich, and the generous layer of salted caramel ganache makes it simply decadent.

INGREDIENTS

For the cake

1½ cups jowar flour
¾ cup cocoa powder
A pinch of salt
1 teaspoon baking powder
½ teaspoon baking soda
¾ cup vegetable oil
1½ cups caster sugar
2 eggs
½ teaspoon vanilla extract
¾ cup milk

For the topping

1 cup whipped salted caramel ganache (see p. 147)
Crushed nuts

METHOD

1. Preheat the oven to 180°C. Line a 9x13-inch pan with parchment paper.

2. In a bowl, whisk together the flour, cocoa powder, salt, baking powder and baking soda, and set aside.

3. In a large bowl, beat the oil and sugar until the mixture is pale. Add the eggs, one at a time and mix well after each addition. Add the vanilla.

4. Fold the dry ingredients into the wet ingredients, starting and ending with the flour mixture and alternating with the milk. Mix until everything is combined and no flour pockets are visible. Do not overmix.

5. Pour the batter into the prepared pan and bake for 35–40 minutes, or until a skewer inserted in the centre of the cake comes out clean. Cool the cake on a wire rack.

6. Frost the cooled cake with the whipped salted caramel ganache and garnish with crushed nuts of your choice.

MINI CHOCOLATE ALMOND BUNDT CAKES

Chocolate and almonds is a classic combination. No one can resist these adorable portions of deliciousness!

INGREDIENTS

1 cup almond flour

¼ cup cocoa powder

1 teaspoon baking powder

½ cup butter

½ cup chopped

dark chocolate

3 eggs, separated

1 cup caster sugar, divided

Salted caramel to drizzle

METHOD

1. Preheat the oven to 180°C. Grease a 6-hole mini Bundt tray with butter.

2. In a bowl, combine the almond flour, cocoa powder and baking powder, and set aside.

3. Take the butter and chocolate in a saucepan over medium heat, and melt, stirring frequently, until combined.

4. In a bowl, whisk the egg yolks and ½ cup sugar until pale. Gradually add the chocolate mixture and combine using a spatula.

5. Fold the dry ingredients into the chocolate mix.

6. In another bowl, whisk the egg whites until they form soft peaks. With the mixer still running, slowly add the remaining ½ cup sugar, whisking until the meringue becomes glossy.

7. Add half of the meringue mixture to the chocolate mix and gently fold to combine. Repeat with the remaining meringue.

8. Pour the batter into the prepared tray and bake for 15–20 minutes, or until a skewer inserted into the cakes comes out clean.

9. Drizzle the Bundt cakes with salted caramel.

CHOCOLATE PEAR CAKE

When you are craving the comfort of a chocolate cake, but want to make it fancy, this is the cake I recommend! Fresh pears go incredibly well with this decadent chocolate sponge.

INGREDIENTS

1½ cups all-purpose flour

¾ cup cocoa powder

½ teaspoon baking soda

1 teaspoon baking powder

1 teaspoon cinnamon powder

½ teaspoon nutmeg powder

½ teaspoon ginger powder

Zest of 1 orange

¾ cup vegetable oil

1½ cups caster sugar

2 eggs

½ teaspoon vanilla extract

¾ cup milk

3 whole pears, peeled

METHOD

1. Preheat the oven to 180°C. Line a 9-inch round cake pan with parchment paper.

2. In a bowl, combine the flour, cocoa powder, baking soda, baking powder, cinnamon powder, nutmeg powder, ginger powder and orange zest, and set aside.

3. In another bowl, beat the oil and sugar until the mixture is light and pale. Add the eggs, one at a time, mixing well after each addition. Add the vanilla extract.

4. Fold the dry ingredients into the wet ingredients, starting and ending with the flour mixture, and alternating with the milk. Mix until everything is just combined and there are no flour pockets in the batter. Do not overmix.

5. Pour the batter into the prepared pan and place the pears in the batter. Bake for 35–40 minutes, or until a skewer inserted in the centre of the cake comes out clean.

MANGO CAKE

I love eating and baking with mangoes, and if there's one cake I could eat all summer,
it would be this one! Moist, fluffy and bursting with flavour!

INGREDIENTS

For the cake

2 cups all-purpose flour

2 teaspoons baking powder

½ teaspoon baking soda

½ cup vegetable oil

1 cup caster sugar

1 cup mango puree

1 teaspoon vanilla extract

¼ cup milk

For the topping

1 cup cream cheese frosting
(see p. 139)

1 cup cubed mangoes

½ cup freeze-dried
raspberries

METHOD

1. Preheat the oven to 180°C. Line a 9-inch round cake pan with parchment paper.

2. In a bowl, combine the flour, baking powder and baking soda, and set aside.

3. In another bowl, beat together the oil and sugar until the mixture is pale. Add the mango puree and vanilla to the oil and sugar mixture. Mix together and combine everything.

4. Fold the dry ingredients into the wet ingredients in three batches, beginning and ending with the flour mixture, and alternating with the milk. Do not overmix.

5. Pour the batter into the prepared pan and bake for 40–45 minutes, or until a skewer inserted in the centre of the cake comes out clean.

6. Allow the cake to cool on a wire rack.

7. Unmould the cooled cake, top with the cream cheese frosting and decorate with cubed mangoes and freeze-dried raspberries.

GRAPEFRUIT POPPY SEED LOAF CAKE

Poppy seeds add a unique nutty element to desserts, and trust me, nothing can substitute their distinctive taste. This cake combines the beauty of grapefruit and the crunch of poppy seeds in a light and airy loaf. I think the poppy seeds are the real hero here; they give the loaf a beautiful speckled look and make it stand out.

INGREDIENTS

For the cake

1½ cups all-purpose flour

2 teaspoons baking powder

½ teaspoon baking soda

1 teaspoon grapefruit zest

½ cup vegetable oil

1 cup caster sugar

3 eggs

2 tablespoons fresh grapefruit juice

½ cup whole milk

¼ cup poppy seeds

For the topping

1 cup whipped cream

Fresh grapefruit slices

METHOD

1. Preheat the oven to 180°C. Line a 9x4-inch loaf pan with parchment paper.

2. In a bowl, combine the flour, baking powder, baking soda and grapefruit zest.

3. In another bowl, beat the oil and sugar together. Add the eggs, one at a time, beating well after each addition. Mix in the grapefruit juice.

4. Fold the dry ingredients into the wet ingredients, beginning and ending with the flour mixture, and alternating with the milk. Mix until everything is just combined. Do not overmix. Fold in the poppy seeds.

5. Pour the batter into the prepared loaf pan. Bake for 30–40 minutes, or until a skewer inserted into the centre of the cake comes out clean.

6. Decorate the cooled cake with whipped cream and fresh grapefruit slices.

HAZELNUT PRALINE BABKA

Babka is a sweet yeast cake that requires a lot of love and a little bit of patience to make. Nothing comes close to the joy of seeing your dough rise and double up, except the moment when you cut into the fluffy babka with its layers of hazelnut praline.

INGREDIENTS

For the dough

½ cup milk
¼ cup caster sugar
¾ tablespoon active dry yeast
¼ cup butter, melted
2 eggs
2⅓ cups all-purpose flour
1 egg, lightly beaten, mixed with 1 tablespoon milk, for the egg wash

For the hazelnut praline filling

⅓ cup granulated sugar
⅓ cup whole hazelnuts, skinned
¼ cup powdered sugar
⅓ cup cocoa powder
½ cup melted dark chocolate
¼ cup melted butter

METHOD

1. Take the milk in a saucepan and heat it until it is lukewarm. Take the saucepan off the heat and add the caster sugar and yeast to the lukewarm milk. Let it sit undisturbed in a warm place for 10 minutes until the mixture becomes foamy.

2. Transfer the mixture to the bowl of a stand mixer, or any large bowl, and add the melted butter and eggs to it. Mix the wet ingredients together using the hook attachment of the mixer or a spoon.

3. Gradually add the flour and continue kneading till the dough comes together. Knead for another 5 minutes and then transfer the dough to a large clean bowl, greased with butter or vegetable oil. Allow the dough to rest in a warm, dry place for 2 hours, or until it doubles in size.

4. To make the praline filling, take the granulated sugar in a saucepan and set it over medium heat. Caramelize until it turns amber in colour. Take the saucepan off the heat and add the hazelnuts to the caramel. Stir, so that caramel coats them evenly. Once the hazelnuts have cooled, transfer them to a food processor and process them until they acquire a crumb-like texture.

5. In a bowl, combine the powdered sugar, cocoa powder, melted chocolate and butter. The

consistency should be spreadable, not runny. Add the hazelnut praline to this mixture and mix well.

6. Check the dough. Once it has risen, transfer it to a lightly floured surface and roll it out into a 15x9-inch rectangle.

7. Spread an even layer of the filling on the dough and roll it into a cylinder, lengthwise.

8. Using a sharp knife, cut the cylinder into two, lengthwise, and cross the two lengths over each other to form a braid.

9. Preheat the oven to 200°C. Line a 9x4-inch loaf pan with parchment paper.

10. Transfer the braided dough into the loaf pan and allow it to proof for another 30 minutes before baking.

11. Once the dough has become puffy, brush the babka with the egg wash and bake it for 30–35 minutes or until the babka is golden brown.

LEMON LAVENDER BUNDT CAKE

I was quite sceptical about the combination of lemon and lavender in a cake, but I decided to listen to the baking gods. I was pleasantly surprised by how delicious this cake turned out to be. I knew I just had to put it in the book. I bake this cake in a Bundt pan for a touch of elegance and top it with a quick and easy lemon glaze for extra grace!

INGREDIENTS

For the cake

4 cups all-purpose flour
4 teaspoons baking powder
½ teaspoon salt
1 tablespoon lemon zest
1½ cups vegetable oil
2 cups caster sugar
1½ teaspoons lavender extract
4 eggs
½ cup milk
8 tablespoons lemon juice

For the glaze

1 cup icing sugar
2 tablespoons lemon juice

METHOD

1. Preheat the oven to 180°C. Generously grease a 9-inch Bundt pan.

2. In a bowl, whisk together the flour, baking powder, salt and lemon zest, and set aside.

3. In another bowl, beat the oil and sugar until the mixture is pale. Add the lavender extract. Add the eggs, one at a time, beating well after each addition. Mix in the milk and lemon juice.

4. Fold the dry ingredients into the wet ingredients. Mix until just combined. Do not overmix.

5. Pour the batter into the Bundt pan. Bake for 45–50 minutes, or until a skewer inserted into the cake comes out clean.

6. To make the lemon glaze, sift the icing sugar into a bowl to remove any lumps. Whisk in the lemon juice until you get the desired consistency. It should be thick, yet pourable.

7. Once the cake has cooled, pour the lemon glaze over it.

COOKIE DOUGH CAKE

My favourite cake to bake for my birthday every year is this one, because nothing makes me happier than a jumbo cookie cake topped with chocolate chips, whipped cream and sprinkles.

INGREDIENTS

For the cake

1⅔ cups all-purpose flour
¾ teaspoon baking soda
1 cup butter
½ cup brown sugar
½ cup caster sugar
2 eggs
1 teaspoon vanilla extract
¼ cup milk
1 cup chocolate chips

For the topping

½ cup whipped cream
Sprinkles

METHOD

1. Preheat the oven to 180°C. Line a 9-inch cake pan with parchment paper.

2. In a bowl, combine the flour and baking soda, and set aside.

3. In another bowl, beat the butter, brown sugar and caster sugar together until the mixture is light and fluffy. Whisk in the eggs, one at a time, and add the vanilla extract.

4. Gently fold the dry ingredients into the wet ingredients and mix until combined. Add the milk and mix until the dough comes together. Add some of the chocolate chips and mix well.

5. Spread the cookie dough into the prepared cake pan. Sprinkle the remaining chocolate chips on top and gently press them down into the dough.

6. Bake for 25–30 minutes, or until the edges become golden brown.

7. Let the cookie dough cake cool completely before turning it out. Decorate it with whipped cream and sprinkles.

LIME RASPBERRY FINANCIERS

A financier is a small, light and moist French cake that contains almond flour or any other form of almond flavouring. I throw in a few more ingredients, like lime and raspberries, to give this simple recipe a fruity twist. You'll fall in love with the fresh, delicious taste of these financiers.

INGREDIENTS

¼ cup all-purpose flour

½ cup ground almonds with skin (or almond meal/flour)

¾ cup icing sugar, sifted

1 teaspoon kafir lime zest

3 egg whites

½ cup butter, melted and cooled

½ teaspoon pure vanilla extract

½ cup fresh raspberries

¼ cup almond flakes

METHOD

1. Preheat the oven to 180°C. Lightly grease a mini cupcake pan with butter.

2. In a bowl, whisk together the flour, ground almonds, icing sugar and kafir lime zest, and set aside.

3. In another bowl, beat the eggs whites until they form soft peaks.

4. Gently fold the dry ingredients into the egg whites, alternating with the melted butter. Mix in the vanilla extract.

5. Transfer the batter to the mini cupcake pan using an ice cream scoop. Top with fresh raspberries and almond flakes.

6. Bake the financiers for 15–20 minutes, or until they are brown on the edges.

WHOLEWHEAT CHERRY CAKE WITH COFFEE CRUMBLE

It's incredible how a well-made crumble topping can significantly enhance a dessert. Topping my cherry cake with a coffee crumble was one of the best baking decisions I ever made! I can have this cake for breakfast, with evening tea, or before dinner. Basically, all the time – it's that good!

INGREDIENTS

For the cake

2 cups wholewheat flour

2 teaspoons baking powder

¼ teaspoon salt

¾ cup vegetable oil

1 cup caster sugar

1 teaspoon vanilla extract

3 eggs

1 cup milk

1 cup pitted cherries

For the crumble

1 cup all-purpose flour

½ cup butter

¼ cup brown sugar

¼ cup granulated white sugar

1 tablespoon coffee powder

1 teaspoon cinnamon

METHOD

1. Preheat the oven to 180°C. Line an 8-inch round cake pan with parchment paper.

2. In a bowl, sift together the flour, baking powder and salt, and set aside.

3. In a large bowl, beat the oil and sugar until the mixture is pale. Add the vanilla, then add the eggs, one at a time, mixing well after each addition.

4. Gently fold the dry ingredients into the wet ingredients in three batches, beginning and ending with the flour mixture, and alternating with the milk. Mix until everything is just combined. Do not overmix. Gently fold the pitted cherries into the batter, reserving some for the top.

5. Pour the batter into the prepared cake pan. Top with the remaining cherries.

6. To make the coffee crumble, combine the flour, butter, brown sugar, granulated sugar, coffee powder and cinnamon in a bowl to form a coarse, crumbly mixture.

7. Sprinkle this coarse mixture evenly over the batter in the baking pan. Bake for 40–45 minutes or until a skewer inserted into the centre of the cake comes out clean.

PLUM QUINOA CAKE

Imagine biting into a cake that almost melts in your mouth and is super healthy too. It's a win–win! The next time someone says that healthy desserts are not tasty, give them a slice of this cake and watch their jaws drop in amazement!

INGREDIENTS

½ cup uncooked quinoa

1 cup water

1 cup wholewheat flour

½ teaspoon cinnamon powder

4 teaspoons baking powder

⅓ cup vegetable oil

½ cup caster sugar

3 eggs

1 teaspoon vanilla extract

⅓ cup plus 4 tablespoons milk

7–10 plums, sliced

METHOD

1. Preheat the oven to 180°C. Line a 9x13-inch rectangular cake pan with parchment paper.

2. Rinse the quinoa under running water. Combine the quinoa and water in a saucepan over medium heat. Bring the mixture to a boil, then lower the heat and cook for 15 minutes. Turn the heat off, let the quinoa sit uncovered for 5 minutes. Fluff it up using a fork. Set aside to cool.

3. In a large bowl, whisk the wholewheat flour, cinnamon powder and baking powder, and set aside.

4. In another bowl, beat the oil and sugar until pale. Add the eggs, one at a time, mixing well after each addition. Add the vanilla extract and milk and mix well.

5. Fold the dry ingredients into the wet ingredients, mixing until just combined. Do not overmix. Add the boiled quinoa to the mixture.

6. Transfer the batter into the prepared baking pan and arrange the plum slices on top.

7. Bake for 30–35 minutes, or until a skewer inserted in the centre of the cake comes out clean.

PISTACHIO AND JAGGERY MINI CAKES

What says 'festive' more than a pistachio cake? These pistachio and jaggery mini cakes are my favourite go-to dessert during Diwali. It's amazing how easy it is to make such a fancy dessert with ingredients lying right there in your kitchen. It's simple, yet delicious and rich – thanks to good ol' jaggery!

INGREDIENTS

For the cake

1½ cups ground pistachios
2 cups wholewheat flour
4 teaspoons baking powder
½ teaspoon cardamom powder
¼ teaspoon ginger powder
1 cup butter
1 cup powdered jaggery
2 teaspoons vanilla extract
6 large eggs (or 2 cups Greek yogurt)
1 cup whole milk

For the topping

1 cup mascarpone cheese
Crushed pistachios

METHOD

1. Preheat the oven to 180°C. Grease 6 mini cake moulds or an 8-inch cake pan with butter.

2. In a bowl, combine the ground pistachios, wholewheat flour, baking powder, cardamom powder and ginger powder, and set aside.

3. In another bowl, beat the butter and jaggery until well combined. Add the eggs, one at a time (or Greek yogurt), followed by the vanilla extract. Mix well.

4. Fold the dry ingredients into the wet ingredients in three batches, beginning and ending with the flour mixture, and alternating with the milk. Mix until just combined. Do not overmix.

5. Using an ice cream scoop, transfer the batter into the prepared tray. Bake for 20–25 minutes, or until a skewer inserted in the centre of the cakes comes out clean. Allow the cakes to cool down completely before unmoulding.

6. Top them with the mascarpone cheese and chopped pistachios.

HONEY FIG CHEESECAKE

I never thought I'd like an eggless cheesecake so much until I had a bite of this one.
This honey fig cheesecake is perfect for a special day and is sure to wow your guests!

INGREDIENTS

For the crust

1¾ cups crushed digestive
biscuits
½ cup butter, melted
2 tablespoons cocoa powder

For the filling

1½ cups cream cheese,
softened
½ cup heavy cream
¼ cup honey
¾ cup sweetened
condensed milk
1 tablespoon lemon juice
2 teaspoons vanilla extract
1½ tablespoons cornflour
Fresh figs, to top

METHOD

1. Preheat the oven to 180°C. Lightly grease a
   6-inch round springform pan and line it with
   parchment paper.

2. To make the crust, combine the crushed digestive
   biscuits, melted butter and cocoa powder in a mixing
   bowl. Press the mixture down into the base of the
   springform pan. Bake the crust for 10 minutes then
   remove it from the oven and let it cool completely.

3. Lower the temperature of the oven to 160°C.

4. For the filling, whip together the cream cheese
   and heavy cream until smooth, using either an
   electric mixer or a hand whisk. Do not incorporate
   any air in the mixture. Add the honey and whisk
   until incorporated. Gradually mix in the sweetened
   condensed milk, lemon juice, vanilla extract and
   cornflour, whisking till everything is combined,
   and there are no lumps. Pour this mixture over the
   cooled crust and gently tap the pan to remove any
   air bubbles.

5. Place the springform pan in a deeper tray filled
   with hot water up to 1 inch, to create a water bath.
   This will ensure that the cheesecake bakes slowly
   and evenly. Bake the cheesecake for 45–50 minutes
   or until the filling starts to set around the edge.
   The centre might seem wobbly but it will continue
   to cook as the cheesecake cools.

6. Remove the cheesecake from the oven and allow it to
   come to room temperature. Refrigerate it for at least
   4 hours or preferably overnight before unmoulding.

7. Top with fresh figs and serve.

PISTACHIO LOAF CAKE

I use a lot of nuts in my recipes; there are so many flavours you can pair with them, the possibilities are endless. I love working with pistachios – they're beautiful and lend great flavour and texture to a cake. This loaf cake is perfect for your evening tea and midnight cravings.

INGREDIENTS

2 cups all-purpose flour

1 cup ground pistachios

2 teaspoons lemon zest

1 teaspoon baking powder

1 teaspoon baking soda

1 cup butter

1 cup caster sugar

4 eggs

1 teaspoon vanilla extract

1 cup milk

METHOD

1. Preheat the oven to 180°C. Line a 9x4-inch loaf pan with parchment paper.

2. In a bowl, combine the flour, ground pistachios, lemon zest, baking powder and baking soda, and set aside.

3. In another bowl, cream together the butter and sugar until light and fluffy. Add the eggs, one at a time, mixing well after every addition. Add the vanilla extract.

4. Fold the dry ingredients into the wet ingredients in three batches, beginning and ending with the flour mixture, and alternating with the milk. Mix until everything is just combined. Do not overmix.

5. Transfer this batter into the prepared pan and bake for 30–40 minutes, or until a skewer inserted in the centre of the loaf comes out clean. Allow the loaf to cool down completely before unmoulding.

PUMPKIN MOUSSE CAKE

This gorgeous three-layer dessert will be the star of your celebrations this year! I used a chocolate cake base because I already had some on hand and the flavours work perfectly together, but you can make any base you like. A biscuit base will be equally delicious.

INGREDIENTS

For the mousse

2 cups pumpkin puree

1½ cups icing sugar

2 teaspoons cinnamon powder

2–3 drops sun orange colour

2 cups whipped cream

2 teaspoons gelatin powder

5 tablespoons cold water

For the base

1 8-inch chocolate cake
(see p. 14)
OR
1 8-inch biscuit base
(see p. 76)

For the topping

1 cup chocolate ganache
(see p. 140)

METHOD

1. To make the cake, follow steps 1 to 6 on p. 14, using a springform pan. Leave the sponge in the pan. Do not unmould it.

2. To make the mousse, combine the pumpkin puree, icing sugar and cinnamon powder in a bowl, whisking until the sugar dissolves. Add the sun orange colour and mix until you get the desired colour. Gently fold in the whipped cream.

3. In a small bowl, mix the gelatin with the cold water and let it sit for 3–4 minutes. Heat the gelatin for 30 seconds.

4. Gradually add the gelatin to the mousse, mixing well.

5. Transfer the mousse on top of the chocolate cake in an even layer, and refrigerate it overnight.

6. Spread a layer of chocolate ganache over the mousse. Let it set before unmoulding the cake from the pan.

COCONUT LOAF CAKE

Make this light-as-air loaf cake for your not-so-chocolatey and warm coffee days. If you like your loaf cakes to crack on the top like I do, dip a knife in melted butter and run it across the surface of the cake batter in the pan before popping it in the oven.

INGREDIENTS

1½ cups all-purpose flour

¾ cup shredded fresh coconut

2 teaspoons baking powder

½ cup butter

1 cup caster sugar

3 eggs

½ teaspoon vanilla extract

¾ cup whole milk

METHOD

1. Preheat the oven to 180°C. Line an 11x4-inch loaf pan with parchment paper.

2. In a bowl, combine the flour, shredded coconut and baking powder, and set side.

3. In another bowl, beat the butter and sugar until the mixture is light and fluffy. Add the eggs, one at a time, beating well after each addition. Add the vanilla extract. Whisk in the milk.

4. Gently fold the dry ingredients into the wet ingredients in three batches until there are no visible flour pockets. Do not overmix.

5. Pour the batter into the prepared loaf tin.

6. Bake for 30–40 minutes, or until a skewer inserted into the centre comes out clean. Let the cake cool before unmoulding.

LEMON CHEESECAKE CUPS

These precious little lemon cheesecake cups are not only beautiful but also surprise you with the freshness of tangy lemons. I love how the sharp taste of citrus perfectly complements the richness of the gooey, delicious cheesecake.

INGREDIENTS

For the crust

1 cup crushed digestive biscuits
¼ cup butter, melted

For the filling

¾ cup cream cheese
¼ cup heavy cream
½ cup sweetened condensed milk
2 teaspoons vanilla extract
1 lemon, zested
1 tablespoon lemon juice
¾ tablespoons cornflour

For the topping

1 cup whipped cream
Lemon zest

METHOD

1. Line a 6-cupcake pan with cupcake liners (or grease a 6-inch springform pan).

2. To make the crust, combine the crushed digestive biscuits and melted butter in a bowl. Press the mixture down into the base of each cupcake mould. Refrigerate the crust for 10 minutes.

3. Preheat the oven to 160°C.

4. To make the filling, whip together the cream cheese and heavy cream until smooth, using either an electric mixer or a hand whisk. Gradually add the sweetened condensed milk, vanilla extract, lemon zest, lemon juice and cornflour, whisking till everything is combined and there are no lumps. Pour this mixture over the cooled crust and gently tap the pan to remove any air bubbles.

5. Place the cupcake tray in a deeper tray filled with hot water up to 1 inch, to create a water bath. This will ensure that the cheesecakes bake slowly and evenly. Bake the cheesecakes for 15–18 minutes or until the filling starts to set around the edge. The centre might seem wobbly but it will continue to cook as the cheesecakes cool.

6. Remove the cheesecake cups from the oven and allow them to come to room temperature. Refrigerate them for at least 2 hours or preferably overnight before unmoulding.

7. Top with a dollop of whipped cream and lemon zest, and serve.

COFFEE WALNUT CAKE

If you love a hint of coffee in your desserts, then this cake is perfect for you! The crunch of the walnuts takes the classic combination of chocolate and coffee to another level.

INGREDIENTS

For the cake

2¼ cups flour

2 teaspoons baking powder

½ teaspoon baking soda

2 teaspoons cinnamon powder

1¼ cups butter

¾ cup caster sugar

¾ cup brown sugar, lightly packed

4 eggs

1½ teaspoons vanilla extract

½ cup milk

2 tablespoons instant coffee powder mixed in 1 tablespoon water

¾ cup chopped walnuts, plus extra to top

For the frosting

1 cup butter

2½ cups icing sugar

½ cup cocoa powder

2 teaspoons vanilla extract

METHOD

1. Preheat the oven to 180°C. Line three 6-inch round pans with parchment paper.

2. In a bowl, whisk together the flour, baking powder, baking soda and cinnamon powder. Set aside.

3. In another bowl, beat the butter, caster sugar and brown sugar together until light and fluffy. Add the eggs one by one, beating well after each addition. Whisk in the vanilla extract and the instant coffee mixture and combine well.

4. Gently fold the dry ingredients into the wet ingredients and mix until everything is combined and there are no large flour pockets in the batter. Add the chopped walnuts.

5. Transfer the batter into the prepared pans and bake for 25–30 minutes or until a skewer inserted in the centre of the cakes comes out clean. Let the cakes cool on a wire rack before unmoulding.

6. To make the frosting, sift the icing sugar and cocoa powder and set aside.

7. In a large bowl, beat the butter using a mixer until smooth and fluffy. With the mixer still running, gradually add the sifted icing sugar and cocoa powder. Add the vanilla extract and mix well.

8. Generously top a layer of cake with the chocolate frosting. Place another cake layer on top of it and repeat until all the layers are done. Top with walnuts and serve.

WHOLEWHEAT CARROT PECAN LOAF CAKE

There's something about carrot cakes that makes me want to eat them all year round! I love the flavour of cinnamon in this moist carrot cake, and the pecans give it a nice, crunchy texture. If you thought carrot cake with cream cheese frosting is as good as it can get, wait until you try this version with hot toffee sauce. It's fantastic!

INGREDIENTS

For the cake

2 cups wholewheat flour

1 teaspoon baking soda

1½ teaspoons baking powder

1½ teaspoons cinnamon powder

½ teaspoon ginger powder

1½ cups brown sugar

1 cup vegetable oil

4 eggs

2 teaspoons vanilla extract

2½ cups grated carrots

1 cup pecans

For the toffee sauce

½ cup butter

½ cup light brown sugar

½ cup heavy cream

½ tsp vanilla extract

METHOD

1. Preheat the oven to 180°C. Line a 9x4-inch loaf pan with parchment paper.

2. To make the cake, whisk together the flour, baking soda, baking powder, cinnamon powder and ginger powder in a bowl, and set aside.

3. In another bowl, beat the sugar and oil until the mixture is pale. Add the eggs, one at a time, beating well after each addition. Add the vanilla.

4. Fold the dry ingredients into the wet ingredients, mixing until just combined. Do not overmix. Fold in the grated carrots.

5. Transfer the batter into the loaf pan and top it with the pecans.

6. Bake for 35–40 minutes, or until a skewer inserted into the centre of the cake comes out clean. Let the cake cool before unmoulding.

7. To make the toffee sauce, melt the butter and sugar in a saucepan set over medium heat. When the mixture is simmering, whisk in the cream and bring it to a boil, stirring continuously as it will bubble up vigorously. Make sure the cream is at room temperature, not cold. Add the vanilla extract and mix well.

8. Top the cake generously with hot toffee sauce before serving.

cookies

CHOCOLATE THUMBPRINT COOKIES

Let's take a moment to appreciate how cute thumbprint cookies are. And if you still have doubts, I have only two things to say – chocolate and peanut butter!

INGREDIENTS

½ cup butter

½ cup icing sugar

1 cup all-purpose flour

½ cup cocoa powder

½ cup peanut butter, to fill

METHOD

1. Preheat the oven to 180°C. Line a baking tray with parchment paper.

2. In a large bowl, beat the butter and sugar together until the mixture is light and fluffy. Gradually add the flour and cocoa powder until the dough comes together.

3. Divide the dough into 10 even-sized balls and place them on the baking tray. With the tip of your thumb, gently press down on the cookie dough balls to get the shape of thumbprint cookies.

4. Bake the cookies for 15–20 minutes.

5. Remove the tray from the oven. Once the cookies have cooled, transfer the peanut butter into a piping bag and carefully fill the cookies.

6. This recipe makes 12 cookies. They can be stored in an airtight container for up to 10 days.

PEANUT BUTTER PIZOOKIE

A delightful 'pizza–cookie', this peanut butter pizookie is ideal for lazy days when you're craving cookies, but chilling and rolling out the dough seems like too much effort.

INGREDIENTS

1¼ cups all-purpose flour

1 tablespoon cornflour

½ teaspoon baking soda

½ cup butter

½ cup caster sugar

½ cup light brown sugar, packed

½ cup smooth peanut butter

1 teaspoon vanilla extract

¼ cup milk

½ cup chocolate chunks

½ cup pretzels

Sea salt, to top

METHOD

1. Preheat the oven to 180°C.

2. In a bowl, combine the flour, cornflour and baking soda, and set aside.

3. In another bowl, cream the butter, caster sugar and light brown sugar until pale and fluffy. Add the peanut butter and vanilla extract. Mix well.

4. Fold the dry ingredients into the butter and sugar mixture. The dough will be dry at this stage. Gradually add the milk to the dough and mix until it comes together.

5. Transfer the dough to a cast-iron skillet and spread it out evenly. Add the pretzels, chocolate chunks and sea salt on top.

6. Bake for 15–20 minutes, or until the edges of the pizookie become golden brown. You can store the pizookie in an airtight container for up to 3 days and reheat it before eating.

WHOLEWHEAT, OAT AND GINGER COOKIES

These cookies are not just healthy, they're super scrumptious and munch-worthy!
I dare you to not fall in love with them.

INGREDIENTS

½ cup wholewheat flour

1¼ cups rolled oats

½ teaspoon ginger powder

½ teaspoon baking soda

½ cup butter

½ cup caster sugar

½ cup loosely packed
brown sugar

1 egg

METHOD

1. In a medium bowl, whisk together the wholewheat flour, rolled oats, ginger powder and baking soda, and set aside.

2. In a large bowl, beat the butter, caster sugar and brown sugar until combined. Beat in the egg and mix well.

3. Fold the dry ingredients into the wet ingredients, making sure everything is thoroughly combined.

4. Let the cookie dough rest in the refrigerator for at least 15 minutes.

5. Preheat the oven to 180°C. Line a baking tray with parchment paper or a silicone mat.

6. Scoop out equal-sized balls of cookie dough with an ice cream scoop and place them on the prepared tray. Gently press them down to flatten them. Space out the cookies because they will spread in the oven.

7. Bake for 10–15 minutes, until the edges are golden brown. Let the cookies rest on the tray for at least 15 minutes before removing them.

8. This recipe makes 10 cookies. They can be stored in an airtight container for 10 days.

BROOKIES

These brookies are my go-to stressbusters on tough, hectic days. The gooey and fudgy texture of these brownie cookies makes all the tiredness disappear. I promise this recipe will lift your mood and make your heart smile.

INGREDIENTS

1½ cups dark chocolate

½ cup butter

1 cup all-purpose flour

3 tablespoons cocoa powder

1 teaspoon baking powder

2 eggs

¾ cup caster sugar

½ cup light brown sugar

Sea salt, to top

METHOD

1. Preheat the oven to 180°C. Line a baking tray with parchment paper or a silicone mat.

2. Melt the chocolate and butter in a saucepan set over medium heat. Keep stirring continuously to make sure the chocolate doesn't burn. Once the chocolate and butter have melted, take the saucepan off the heat and allow the mixture to cool.

3. In another bowl, combine the flour, cocoa powder and baking powder.

4. In a large bowl, whisk together the eggs, caster sugar and light brown sugar using an electric mixer until pale and fluffy. Add the cooled chocolate mixture and mix well.

5. Fold the dry ingredients into the wet ingredients.

6. Using an ice-cream scoop, scoop out equal-sized balls of the brownie mixture onto the prepared baking tray. Keep sufficient space between them as they will spread. Bake for 15–17 minutes. Let them cool on the tray before removing them. Sprinkle some sea salt on top.

7. Eat these immediately or store them in an airtight container for up to 2 weeks.

NO-BAKE CHOCOLATE COOKIES

Cookies are one of the easiest things to make. And this recipe doesn't even require you to switch your oven on! All you lazy bakers out there, this one is for you.

INGREDIENTS

½ cup butter

1¼ cups granulated sugar

½ cup milk

¼ cup unsweetened cocoa powder

½ cup creamy peanut butter

1 teaspoon vanilla extract

2 cups rolled oats

METHOD

1. Combine the butter, sugar, milk and cocoa powder in a saucepan set over medium heat. Keep stirring until the butter is completely melted. Bring the mixture to a boil and then take it off the heat.

2. Stir in the peanut butter and vanilla extract, and whisk until combined. Add the oats and mix until they are completely coated with the chocolate and peanut butter mixture.

3. Refrigerate the dough for 1 hour so that it begins to set.

4. Once the dough has chilled completely, portion it out into equal-sized pieces using an ice cream scoop. Roll them into balls and press them gently with your fingers to shape them like cookies.

5. This recipe makes 12–15 cookies. They can be stored in an airtight container for up to 10 days.

EDIBLE CHOCOLATE CHIP COOKIE DOUGH BALLS

I made these dough balls often in college. When exam prep left little time for me to spend in the kitchen but baking therapy was much needed, these simple, no-bake dough balls always came to my rescue.

INGREDIENTS

1¼ cups all-purpose flour

½ cup unsalted butter

½ cup peanut butter

½ cup light brown sugar, packed

⅓ cup caster sugar

1½ tablespoons milk

1 teaspoon vanilla extract

¾ cup milk chocolate chips

METHOD

1. Preheat the oven to 180°C degrees.

2. Spread the flour evenly on a baking sheet. Bake for 5 minutes, then remove from the oven and cool completely. You can also roast it lightly on the stovetop.

3. In a bowl, cream the butter, peanut butter, brown sugar and caster sugar until pale and fluffy. Whisk in the milk and vanilla extract. Fold in the flour. Add the chocolate chips (reserve some if you want to press them on the cookie dough balls later) and mix well. Let the dough rest in the refrigerator for at least 30 minutes.

4. Scoop out equal-sized balls of the chilled dough and roll them between your palms to get a smooth finish. Press the reserved chocolate chips onto the dough balls.

5. Serve the cookie dough balls immediately or store them in an airtight container in the refrigerator.

6. This recipe makes 10 cookie dough balls.

ANZAC COOKIES

Anzac is a sweet biscuit that's popular in Australia and New Zealand. Made with rolled oats, coconut and maple syrup, these cookies are very different from the ones I usually make.

INGREDIENTS

1 cup rolled oats

1 cup wholewheat flour

¾ cup shredded coconut

¾ cup caster sugar

½ cup butter

4 tablespoons maple syrup

1½ teaspoons baking soda

6 tablespoons boiling water

METHOD

1. Preheat the oven to 180°C. Lightly grease a baking tray and line it with parchment paper or a silicon mat.

2. In a bowl, combine the rolled oats, wholewheat flour, shredded coconut and caster sugar.

3. Melt the butter and maple syrup in a small saucepan over medium heat until the mixture is bubbling. Take it off the heat.

4. In another bowl, combine the baking soda and boiling water. The mixture should bubble up. Add this to the hot butter.

5. Combine the butter mixture with the dry ingredients to form a dough.

6. Scoop out equal-sized balls of cookie dough using an ice cream scoop and place them on the baking tray. Keep in mind the cookies will spread as they bake.

7. Bake the cookies for 13–15 minutes, until they're a deep golden brown colour. Allow them to cool on the tray before removing them.

8. This recipe makes 10 cookies. They can be stored for up to 10 days in an airtight container.

PISTACHIO AND WHITE CHOCOLATE COOKIES

These incredibly soft and buttery pistachio and white chocolate cookies are bound to become your new favourite. Each bite brings with it an explosion of textures and flavours. You won't be able to resist reaching out for another piece even before you've finished the one in your hand!

INGREDIENTS

½ cup butter

½ cup light brown sugar, packed

½ cup caster sugar

1 egg (or 1 tablespoon ground flax seeds mixed with 3 tablespoons water, rested for 5 minutes)

1 teaspoon vanilla extract

1¼ cups all-purpose flour

½ teaspoon baking soda

¼ teaspoon cardamom powder

2 tablespoons milk

½ cup white chocolate chunks

¼ cup chopped pistachios

METHOD

1. In a large bowl, cream the butter, brown sugar and caster sugar until light and fluffy. Beat in the egg (or the flax seed mixture), then add the vanilla extract.

2. Fold in the flour, baking soda and cardamom powder. Slowly add the milk to bring the dough together. Refrigerate the cookie dough for at least 1 hour.

3. Preheat the oven to 180°C. Line a baking tray with parchment paper or a silicone mat.

4. Scoop out equal-sized balls of the dough with a spoon or ice cream scoop and place them on the prepared baking tray. Gently press down on the dough balls with your fingers to flatten them a little. Top with the white chocolate chunks and pistachios.

5. Bake the cookies for 12–15 minutes, or until the edges turn golden brown. Let the cookies cool on the tray before removing them.

6. This recipe makes 6 cookies. They can be stored in an airtight container for up to 10 days.

LEMON CRINKLE COOKIES

If you're looking for a cookie that's easy and super fun to make, tastes delicious and packs a lemony punch, then this is the recipe for you!

INGREDIENTS

1½ cups all-purpose flour

1 teaspoon baking powder

¼ cup butter

½ cup caster sugar

1 egg

1½ tablespoons lemon juice

1–2 drops of yellow food colouring

¼ cup powdered sugar, to coat

METHOD

1. In a bowl, whisk together the flour and baking powder.

2. In another bowl, cream the butter and sugar until fluffy. Add the egg and lemon juice, and mix well. Add 1–2 drops of yellow food colouring.

3. Combine the dry ingredients with the wet ingredients until the dough comes together. Cover the dough in plastic wrap and refrigerate it for 30 minutes.

4. Preheat the oven to 180°C. Line a cookie sheet or baking tray with parchment paper.

5. Make 1–1.5-inch balls out of the cookie dough and roll them in the powdered sugar before placing them on the baking tray. Bake for 15–20 minutes. Let the cookies cool on the tray before removing them.

6. This recipe makes 10–12 cookies. They can be stored in an airtight container for up to 7 days.

SHORTBREAD COOKIES

These classic melt-in-the-mouth cookies are super easy to make and require the most basic ingredients. Top them with Nutella, sprinkle some sea salt and you have a delicious treat on your hands!

INGREDIENTS

1 cup butter

½ cup caster sugar

1 teaspoon vanilla extract

2 cups all-purpose flour

Nutella and sea salt, to top

METHOD

1. Preheat the oven to 180°C. Line a baking tray with parchment paper.

2. In a bowl, beat the butter and sugar until fluffy. Add the vanilla extract. Add flour and mix well until the dough comes together. If the dough is too soft, cover it with plastic wrap and refrigerate it until it hardens enough to work with.

3. Roll out the dough into a circle, ¼ inch thick.

4. Use a cookie cutter to cut the dough into the desired shapes.

5. Bake the cookies for 10–12 minutes, or until the edges become golden brown. Let them cool completely before trying to lift them off the tray.

6. Top them with some Nutella and sea salt for added flavour.

7. This recipe makes 15–20 cookies.

VEGAN CHOCOLATE-CHIP COOKIES

I really wanted to include a chocolate chip cookie recipe for my vegan readers. This recipe uses no dairy, but the result is a rich and flavourful chocolate chip cookie with a texture to die for.

INGREDIENTS

1 cup all-purpose flour

½ cup coconut sugar

3 tablespoons cocoa powder

½ teaspoon baking soda

4 tablespoons almond milk

2 tablespoons vegetable oil

1 teaspoon vanilla extract

⅓ cup vegan chocolate chips

METHOD

1. Preheat the oven at 180°C. Line a baking tray with a silicon mat or parchment paper.

2. In a large bowl, combine the flour, coconut sugar, cocoa powder and baking soda. Add the almond milk, oil and the vanilla extract. Keep mixing until you achieve the consistency of cookie dough. Let the dough rest in the refrigerator for 1 hour.

3. Scoop out equal-sized balls of the dough using an ice cream scoop and set them on the baking tray, keeping enough space between them. Flatten the cookies with your fingers and gently press the chocolate chips into place. Sprinkle the sea salt on top.

4. Bake the cookies for 15–20 minutes. Let them rest on the baking tray for 10 minutes before you remove them.

5. This recipe makes 10 cookies. They can be stored in an airtight container for up to 7 days.

CHOCOLATE CHUNK AND PECAN COOKIE BARS

A square of perfectly baked brown butter cookie dough with molten chunks of dark chocolate and crunchy pecan nuts – that, right there, is happiness in a bite.

INGREDIENTS

1 cup butter
½ cup caster sugar
½ cup light brown sugar, packed
2¼ cups all-purpose flour
1 teaspoon baking soda
4 tablespoons milk
½ cup chocolate chunks
½ cup pecans
Sea salt, to top

METHOD

1. Melt the butter in a saucepan set over medium heat and allow it to foam, stirring continuously. Once the butter has changed colour and become brown, take it off the heat and let it cool.

2. In a large bowl, combine the browned butter, caster sugar and light brown sugar using a spatula. Fold in the flour and baking soda. Slowly add the milk to bring the dough together. Refrigerate the prepared dough for at least 1 hour.

3. Preheat the oven to 180°C. Line a 9x9-inch pan with parchment paper, leaving an overhang on at least two sides to help lift the bars off the pan.

4. Spread the cookie dough in the prepared pan, and top with chocolate chunks and pecans.

5. Bake for 20 minutes, or until the cookie turns golden brown. Sprinkle some sea salt on top. Let the cookie cool completely before cutting it into equal-sized bars.

6. This recipe makes 9 large bars. They can be stored in an airtight container for up to 10 days.

CHOCOLATE ORANGE BISCOTTI

Biscotti is a twice-baked biscuit. These crisp and delicious cookies are the perfect companion for your evening mug of coffee.

INGREDIENTS

1 cup all-purpose flour

½ cup caster sugar

½ teaspoon baking powder

Zest of 1 orange

½ teaspoon vanilla extract

2 tablespoons butter

1 egg

½ cup chocolate chips

METHOD

1. Preheat the oven to 180°C. Line a baking tray with parchment paper and set aside.

2. In a bowl, combine the flour, sugar, baking powder and orange zest. Add the vanilla extract and the butter, and mix until combined. Add the egg and mix until the dough becomes slightly sticky. Now add the chocolate chips.

3. Turn out the dough on to a floured surface and roll it into a log, 7 inches long and 4 inches wide.

4. Carefully transfer the log onto the baking tray and bake for 25–30 minutes, until it forms a hard crust and turns golden brown. Take the log out of the oven and let it cool on a wire rack for 10–15 minutes.

5. Once cooled, transfer the log to a cutting board and using a sharp serrated knife cut it into slices about ¼–½ inch thick. Return the slices to the baking tray and bake for 10 minutes. Turn the slices over and bake for another 10 minutes or until they are firm to touch. Let them cool on the tray before removing them.

6. This recipe makes 12 thin biscotto. They can be stored in an airtight container for up to 10 days.

S'MORES COOKIES

Everybody I know loves chocolate chip cookies. I recommend taking this classic cookie to the next level and turning them into s'mores cookies! Chocolate chunks, marshmallows and biscuits – all mixed into the dough. It's the sugar hug you need!

INGREDIENTS

1½ cups all-purpose flour

½ teaspoon baking soda

¼ teaspoon baking powder

½ cup crushed digestive biscuits

½ cup butter

½ cup brown sugar

1 egg

½ teaspoon vanilla extract

½ cup chocolate chips

½ cup mini marshmallows

METHOD

1. Preheat the oven to 180°C. Line a baking tray with parchment paper.

2. In a bowl, combine the flour, baking soda, baking powder and crushed digestive biscuits. Set aside.

3. In another bowl, beat the butter and brown sugar until the mixture is light and fluffy. Whisk in the egg and add the vanilla.

4. Combine the dry ingredients with the wet ingredients and mix until the dough comes together. Fold in the chocolate chips.

5. Scoop out the dough into equal-sized balls using an ice cream scoop and place them on the prepared tray. Flatten them lightly with your fingers and top them with the marshmallows.

6. Bake the cookies for about 12–15 minutes, or until the edges become golden brown. Let them cool on the baking tray for at least 10 minutes.

7. This recipe makes 6–8 cookies. They can be stored in an airtight container for up to 7 days.

cupcakes & muffins

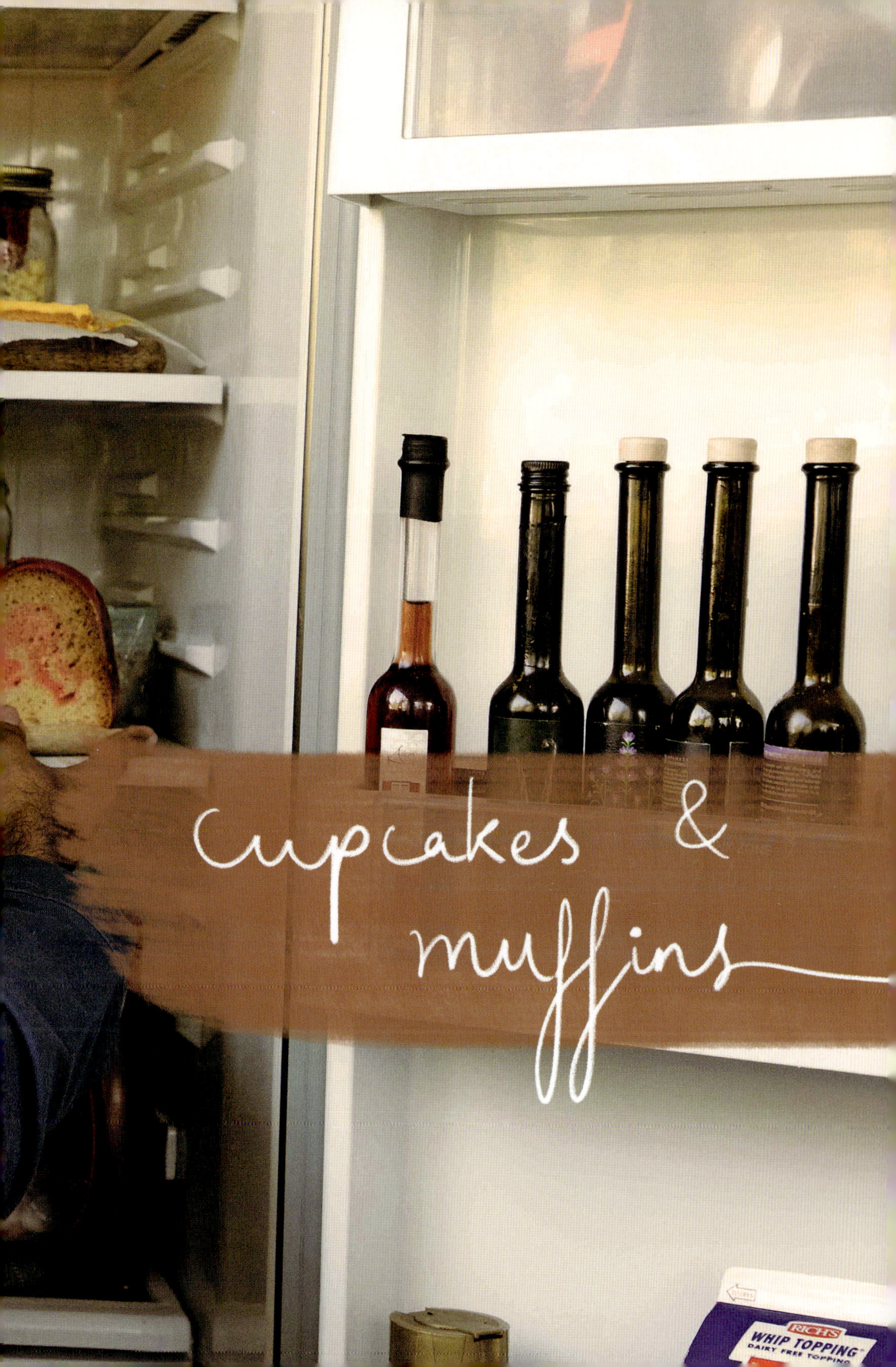

CHOCOLATE CUPCAKES

We all love a good chocolate cupcake that's luscious and decadent. This recipe will give you all that and more! The whipped chocolate ganache on top is the perfect addition to this delectable cupcake.

INGREDIENTS

For the cupcakes

1½ cups all-purpose flour

¾ cup cocoa powder

1 teaspoon baking powder

½ teaspoon baking soda

A pinch of salt

¾ cup vegetable oil

1½ cups caster sugar

1 cup Greek yogurt

½ teaspoon vanilla extract

½ cup milk mixed with
1 teaspoon white vinegar,
rested for 5 minutes

For the topping

1 cup whipped chocolate
ganache (see p. 143)

Fresh raspberries

METHOD

1. Preheat the oven to 180°C. Line a cupcake tray with cupcake liners.

2. In a bowl, sift together the flour, cocoa powder, baking powder, baking soda and salt, and set aside.

3. In another bowl, beat the oil and sugar until the mixture is pale. Add the yogurt and vanilla extract and mix well.

4. Fold the dry ingredients into the wet ingredients, starting and ending with flour mixture, and alternating with the milk. Mix till just combined. Do not overmix.

5. Transfer the batter into the cupcake tray using an ice cream scoop, filling up to ⅔ of the moulds. Make sure to not overfill as the batter might spill over.

6. Bake for 20–25 minutes, or until a skewer inserted in centre of the cupcakes comes out clean.

7. Allow the cupcakes to cool completely before frosting with the whipped ganache and topping with raspberries.

8. This recipe makes 12 cupcakes.

RED VELVET CUPCAKES

There's something about red velvet desserts that just draws you to them. Red velvet and cream cheese is a classic pairing. And these crowd-pleaser cupcakes are guaranteed to be a hit!

INGREDIENTS

For the cupcakes

1½ cups all-purpose flour

2 tablespoons cocoa powder

1 teaspoon baking soda

1 cup caster sugar

½ cup vegetable oil

6 tablespoons Greek yogurt

2 teaspoons lemon juice

2 teaspoons vanilla extract

6–8 teaspoons red food colouring

1½ cup buttermilk (1½ cup milk mixed with 2 tablespoons white vinegar)

For the topping

1 cup cream cheese frosting (see p. 139)

METHOD

1. Preheat the oven to 180°C. Line a cupcake tray with cupcake liners.

2. In a large bowl, combine the flour, cocoa powder and baking soda together, and set aside.

3. In another bowl, beat the sugar and oil until pale. Add the yogurt, lemon juice, vanilla and red colour and mix until everything is well combined.

4. Fold the dry ingredients into the wet ingredients in three batches, beginning and ending with the flour mixture, and alternating with the buttermilk. Mix till everything is just combined and there are no large flour pockets. Do not overmix.

5. Transfer the batter into the prepared cupcake tray using an ice cream scoop, filling up to ⅔ of the moulds. Make sure to not overfill as the batter might spill over. Bake for 20–25 minutes, or until a skewer inserted into the centre of the cupcakes comes out clean.

6. Once the cupcakes have cooled, top them with the cream cheese frosting and decorate with red velvet cupcake crumbs.

7. This recipe makes 12 cupcakes.

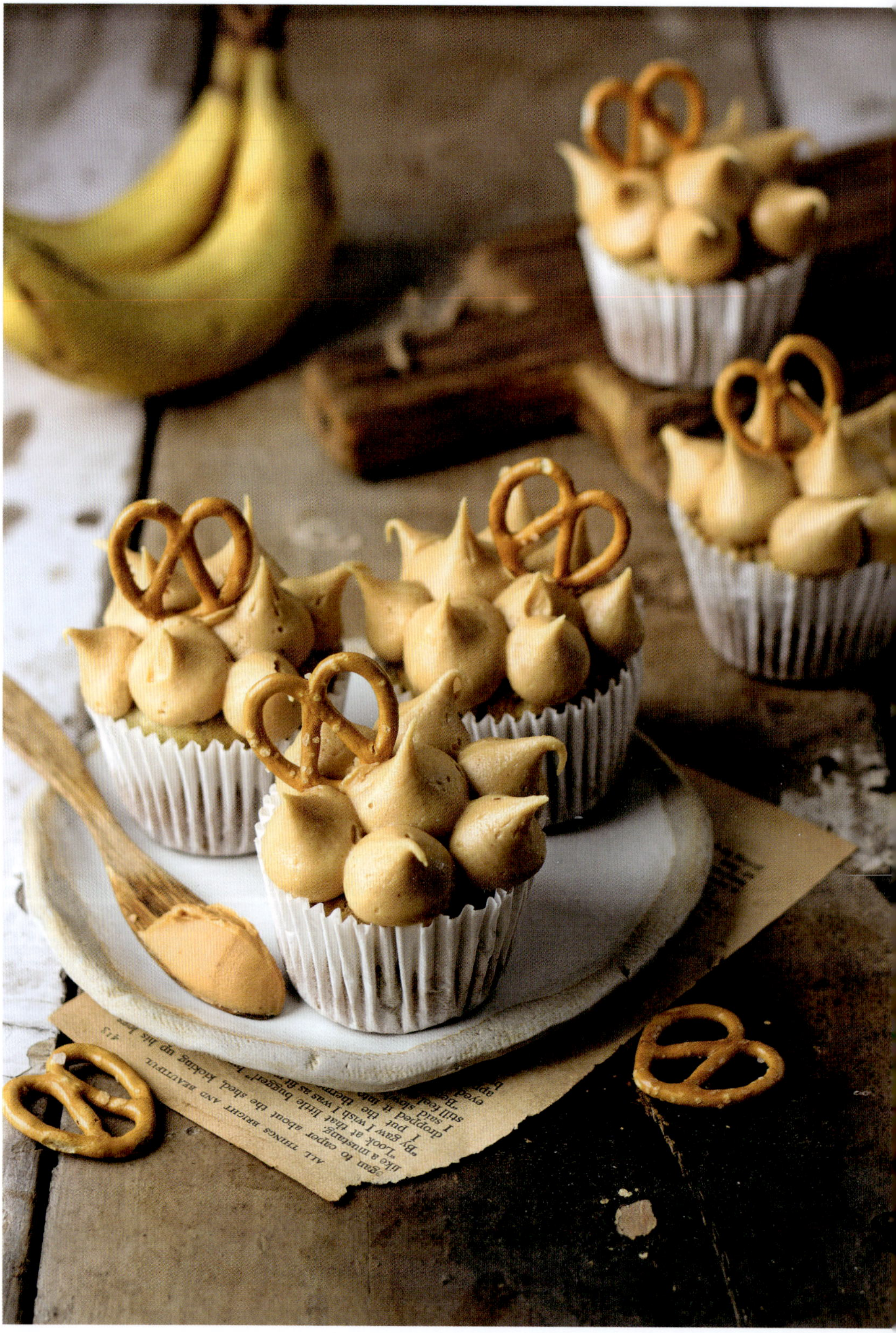

BANANA CUPCAKES WITH PEANUT BUTTER FROSTING

This is one of my favourite cupcake recipes ever. Combining the sweet taste of bananas and the nutty flavour of peanut butter, these cupcakes are the definition of wholesome and I can't wait for you to bake them!

INGREDIENTS

For the cupcakes

¾ cup all-purpose flour

¼ cup caster sugar

¼ teaspoon baking soda

½ teaspoon baking powder

¼ cup vegetable oil

1 large egg

2 ripe bananas, mashed

¼ cup milk

For the frosting

½ cup butter

½ cup smooth peanut butter

½ teaspoon vanilla extract

1½ cups icing sugar, sifted

For the topping

Pretzels

METHOD

1. Preheat the oven to 180°C. Line a cupcake tray with cupcake liners.

2. In a large bowl, combine the flour, sugar, baking soda and baking powder, and set side.

3. In another bowl, beat the oil and the egg until frothy. Whisk in the flour mixture, followed by the mashed bananas. Add the milk and mix well.

4. Transfer the batter into the prepared cupcake tray using an ice cream scoop, filling up to ⅔ of the moulds. Make sure to not overfill as the batter might spill over.

5. Bake for 20 minutes, or until a skewer inserted in the centre of the cupcakes comes out clean. Let them cool.

6. To make the frosting, beat the butter, peanut butter and vanilla together in a large bowl until the mixture is light and fluffy. With the mixer still running, add the icing sugar in batches. Beat until the frosting is smooth and fluffy.

7. Top the cupcakes with the peanut butter frosting and pretzels.

8. This recipe makes 6 cupcakes.

PLUM AND CHIA SEED MUFFINS

I remember being extremely sceptical when I first started using chia seeds in my recipes, but now, I can't get enough of the texture they add to my cakes. Don't forget to add orange zest in these muffins – one bite and you'll know why I never skip this step!

INGREDIENTS

1 cup wholewheat flour

1 cup almond flour

2 teaspoons baking powder

½ teaspoon cinnamon powder

Zest of 1 orange

½ cup olive oil

1 cup light brown sugar

4 eggs

¼ cup milk

2 tablespoons chia seeds

5–6 plums, sliced

½ cup flaked almonds

METHOD

1. Preheat the oven to 180°C. Line a muffin tray with liners.

2. In a bowl, combine the wholewheat flour, almond flour, baking powder, cinnamon powder and orange zest, and set aside.

3. In another bowl, beat the oil and sugar together until the mixture is pale. Add the eggs one at a time, beating well after each addition. Mix in the milk.

4. Fold the dry ingredients into the wet ingredients, mixing until there are no large pockets in the batter. Do not overmix. Add the chia seeds.

5. Transfer the batter into the cupcake liners using an ice cream scoop, filling up to the top of the moulds. Carefully place the plum slices on top and sprinkle the flaked almonds.

6. Bake for 25 minutes, or until a skewer inserted in the centre of the muffins comes out clean.

7. This recipe make 12 muffins.

STRAWBERRY CUPCAKES WITH STRAWBERRY BUTTERCREAM

If you love strawberries as much as I do, then this dessert is for you. The strawberry buttercream on these cupcakes really makes them shine!

INGREDIENTS

For the cupcakes

½ cup all-purpose flour

½ teaspoon baking powder

4 tablespoons butter

⅓ cup caster sugar

1 teaspoon vanilla extract

1 egg (or 2 tablespoons ground flax seeds mixed with 1 tablespoon water, rested for 5 minutes)

4 tablespoons milk

8–10 fresh strawberries, chopped

For the frosting

½ cup strawberries, diced

¼ cup water

1 tablespoon caster sugar

½ tablespoon cornflour mixed in 1 tablespoon water

½ cup butter

1 cup icing sugar

1 teaspoon vanilla extract

METHOD

1. Preheat the oven to 180°C. Prepare a cupcake pan with liners.

2. In a bowl, combine the flour and baking powder.

3. In another bowl, cream the butter, sugar and vanilla extract until the mixture is pale and fluffy. Beat in the egg (or the flax seed mixture).

4. Fold the dry ingredients into the wet ingredients. Add the milk and combine. Do not overmix. Add the strawberries. Transfer the batter into the cupcake pan using an ice cream scoop, filling up to ⅔ of the moulds. Do not overfill as the batter might spill over. Bake for 20–25 minutes, or until a skewer inserted into the cupcakes comes out clean. Let them cool.

5. To make the frosting, cook the strawberries, water and sugar in a saucepan over medium heat for 10 minutes until the strawberries become soft. Add the cornflour paste and cook until the mixture thickens. Chill the strawberry compote in the refrigerator for about 30 minutes, then puree it in a food processor.

6. In a large bowl, whisk the butter until light and fluffy. With the mixer still running, gradually add the icing sugar until fully incorporated. Add the vanilla extract. Mix the strawberry puree into the buttercream using a spatula.

7. Top the cooled cupcakes with the strawberry buttercream frosting.

8. This recipe makes 6 cupcakes.

CARROT COCONUT CUPCAKES

Carrots and coconut is a simply phenomenal combination! The hint of warm ginger in these cupcakes makes them perfect for your winter lunches and Christmas celebrations.

INGREDIENTS

For the cupcakes

1 cup all-purpose flour
¼ cup shredded coconut
½ teaspoon ginger powder
½ teaspoon baking powder
½ cup vegetable oil
¼ cup caster sugar
¼ cup brown sugar
1 teaspoon vanilla extract
1 tablespoon ground
flax seed mixed with
3 tablespoons water,
rested for 5 minutes
¼ cup milk
½ cup grated carrots

For the topping

2 cups cream cheese frosting
(see p. 139)
Crushed pecans

METHOD

1. Preheat the oven to 180°C. Line a cupcake tray with cupcake liners.

2. In a bowl, whisk together the flour, shredded coconut, ginger powder and baking powder, and set aside.

3. In another bowl, beat the oil, caster sugar and brown sugar together. Add the vanilla extract and the flax seed mixture. Beat well. Whisk in the milk.

4. Gently fold the dry ingredients into the wet ingredients. Mix till just combined. Do not overmix. Add the grated carrots and combine gently.

5. Transfer the batter into the prepared cupcake tray using an ice cream scoop, filling up to ⅔ of the moulds. Make sure to not overfill as the batter might spill over. Bake for 20–25 minutes, or until a skewer inserted into the centre of the cupcakes comes out clean.

6. Once the cupcakes have cooled completely, top with the cream cheese frosting and crushed pecans.

7. This recipe makes 6 cupcakes.

CHOCOLATE CHIP MUFFINS WITH CHOCOLATE CRUMBLE

Chocolate chip is one of the most popular flavours around the world. Cookies, cakes, muffins, cupcakes, waffles, pancakes – chocolate chips make everything better! These muffins are so easy to make and require nothing but the most basic ingredients.

INGREDIENTS

For the muffins

2½ cups all-purpose flour

½ cup cocoa powder

1 teaspoon baking soda

1 teaspoon baking powder

½ cup butter

1 cup caster sugar

1 cup milk

2 eggs

1 cup chocolate chips

For the chocolate crumble

¼ cup all-purpose flour

¼ cup caster sugar

¼ cup cold butter, cubed

¼ cup cocoa powder

METHOD

1. Preheat the oven to 180°C. Line a muffin tin with paper liners.

2. In a bowl, combine the flour, cocoa powder, baking soda and baking powder, and set aside.

3. In another bowl, beat the butter and sugar until light and fluffy. Add the eggs, one at a time, beating well after each addition.

4. Fold the dry ingredients into the wet ingredients in three batches, beginning and ending with the flour mixture, and alternating with the milk. Mix until just combined. Do not overmix. Carefully add the chocolate chips, reserving some for the top.

5. To make the crumble, mix the flour, sugar, cold butter and cocoa powder in a bowl until well combined.

6. Transfer the muffin batter into the prepared tray using an ice cream scoop, filling to the top of the moulds. Top with the remaining chocolate chips and chocolate crumble.

7. Bake for 30 minutes, or until a skewer inserted into the centre of the muffins comes out clean.

8. This recipe makes 12 muffins.

MOCHA NUTELLA CUPCAKES

These mocha cupcakes with Nutella frosting are the perfect example
of the heavenly combination of coffee and chocolate.

INGREDIENTS

For the cupcakes

½ cup milk mixed with
1 teaspoon vinegar, rested for
5 minutes
½ cup espresso, lukewarm
1½ cups all-purpose flour
½ cup cocoa powder
1 teaspoon baking soda
½ cup butter
1½ cups caster sugar
2 eggs
2 teaspoons vanilla extract

For the topping

½ cup butter
½ cup Nutella
1½ cup icing sugar
Honeycomb crumbs
(see p. 206; omit the
popcorn)

METHOD

1. Preheat the oven to 180°C. Line a cupcake tray with paper liners.

2. In a small bowl, combine the espresso with the milk and vinegar mixture.

3. In a bowl, whisk the flour, cocoa powder and baking soda together, and set aside.

4. In another bowl, cream the butter and sugar together until light and fluffy. Add the eggs, one at a time, beating well after each addition. Whisk in the vanilla extract.

5. Fold the dry ingredients into the wet ingredients in three batches, beginning and ending with the flour mixture, and alternating with the milk and coffee mixture. Mix until there are no large flour pockets in the batter. Do not overmix.

6. Transfer the batter into the prepared cupcake tray using an ice cream scoop, filling up to ⅔ of the moulds. Make sure to not overfill as the batter might spill over. Bake for 20–25 minutes, or until a skewer inserted into the centre of the cupcakes comes out clean.

7. To make the frosting, beat the butter and Nutella together until the mixture is light and airy. With the mixer still running, add the sugar in batches, beating until the frosting is smooth and fluffy.

8. Once the cupcakes have cooled completely, top them with the frosting and honeycomb crumbs.

9. This recipe makes 12 cupcakes.

STRAWBERRY MUFFINS

It's no secret that strawberries are one of my favourite ingredients. These muffins are my go-to dessert whenever strawberries are in season. These tart–sweet muffins are an absolute winner.

INGREDIENTS

1½ cups all-purpose flour

2 teaspoons baking powder

¼ cup vegetable oil

½ cup caster sugar

1 teaspoon vanilla extract

1 egg (or 1 tablespoon ground flax seeds mixed with 3 tablespoons water, rested for 5 minutes)

½ cup milk

½ cup diced fresh strawberries

METHOD

1. Preheat the oven to 180°C. Line a muffin tray with paper liners.

2. In a bowl, combine the flour and baking powder, and set aside.

3. In another bowl, beat the oil and sugar until the mixture is pale. Add the vanilla extract and the egg and beat well. Mix in the milk.

4. Carefully fold the dry ingredients into the wet ingredients until just combined. Do not overmix. Gently mix in the strawberries, reserving some for the top.

5. Transfer the muffin batter into the paper liners using an ice cream scoop, filling to the top of the moulds. Top with the remaining fresh strawberries.

6. Bake for 25–30 minutes, or until a skewer inserted in the centre of the muffins comes out clean.

7. This recipe makes 6 muffins.

RASPBERRY CUPCAKES

Raspberries are one of my favourite berries to bake with. They're sweet, and have the perfect amount of tartness. These raspberry and cream cheese cupcakes take things to the next level and bring happy smiles all around the dinner table!

INGREDIENTS

For the cupcakes

¾ cup all-purpose flour

1 teaspoon baking powder

¼ teaspoon salt

¼ cup butter

⅓ cup caster sugar

2 eggs

1 teaspoon vanilla extract

2 tablespoons milk

½ cup frozen raspberries

For the topping

2 cups cream cheese frosting (see p. 139)

Fresh raspberries

METHOD

1. Preheat the oven to 180°C. Line a cupcake tray with paper liners.

2. In a bowl, combine the flour, baking powder and salt, and set side.

3. In another bowl, cream the butter and sugar together until light and fluffy. Add the eggs, one at a time, beating well after each addition. Whisk in the vanilla extract.

4. Fold the dry ingredients into the wet ingredients, beginning and ending with the flour mixture, and alternating with the milk. Add the frozen raspberries. Do not overmix.

5. Transfer the batter into the cupcake tray using an ice cream scoop, filling up to ⅔ of the moulds. Make sure to not overfill as the batter might spill over.

6. Bake for 15–20 minutes, until golden brown or until a skewer inserted into the centre of the cupcakes comes out clean.

7. Once the cupcakes have cooled completely, top with the cream cheese frosting and fresh raspberries.

8. This recipe makes 6 cupcakes.

LEMON POPPY SEED CUPCAKES

Lemon is a spectacular flavour and it adds the perfect amount of freshness to any dessert! Add poppy seeds to this equation and you'll find yourself doing a happy dance once you bite into one of these beautiful lemon poppy seed cupcakes.

INGREDIENTS

For the cupcakes

1½ cups all-purpose flour

1 teaspoon baking powder

½ teaspoon baking soda

1 tablespoon lemon zest

¾ cup vegetable oil

1½ cups caster sugar

1 cup Greek yogurt

5 tablespoons lemon juice

½ cup milk

2 tablespoons poppy seeds

For the topping

2 cups cream cheese frosting (see p. 139)

Lemon zest

Poppy seeds

METHOD

1. Preheat the oven to 180°C. Line a cupcake tray with paper liners.

2. In a large bowl, combine the flour, baking powder, baking soda and lemon zest, and set aside.

3. In another bowl, beat the oil and sugar till pale. Add the Greek yogurt and lemon juice, and beat well.

4. Fold the dry ingredients into the wet ingredients in three batches, beginning and ending with the flour mixture, and alternating with the milk. Mix till just combined. Do not overmix. Add the poppy seeds to the batter and combine gently.

5. Transfer the batter into the prepared pan using an ice cream scoop, filling up to ⅔ of the moulds. Make sure to not overfill as the batter might spill over. Bake for 15–20 minutes or until the cupcakes are golden brown and a skewer inserted in the centre comes out clean.

6. Once the cupcakes have cooled, top them with the cream cheese frosting, and sprinkle lemon zest and poppy seeds for added flavour.

7. This recipe makes 6 cupcakes.

frostings & fillings

CREAM CHEESE FROSTING

When it comes to frostings, there are several options, but my personal favourite is cream cheese frosting. From sheet cakes to cupcakes, I can frost anything and everything with it.

INGREDIENTS

1 cup cream cheese, softened
½ cup butter, softened
Beans from half a vanilla pod,
or 1 teaspoon vanilla extract
1½ cups icing sugar, sifted

METHOD

1. In a bowl, beat the cream cheese with the butter until it is light and fluffy. Make sure the butter and cream cheese are well-incorporated and the mixture is smooth. Add the vanilla beans or the extract.

2. With the mixer still running, add the icing sugar in batches. It is necessary to sift the icing sugar as it may contain lumps.

3. Beat the frosting until it is smooth and fluffy.

4. This recipe makes 1 cup of frosting. The frosting can be stored in an airtight container in the refrigerator for 3–4 days.

CHOCOLATE GANACHE

Chocolate ganache is one of the most delicious things to put on desserts. It can elevate a simple dessert into something divine, and even save you from disasters such as cracked cakes. It's my go-to topping because it only needs two ingredients and is ready in no time!

INGREDIENTS

1 cup roughly chopped
dark chocolate
1 cup fresh cream

METHOD

1. Put the dark chocolate in a heatproof bowl.

2. Heat the fresh cream in a saucepan until it begins to simmer. Make sure it doesn't boil.

3. Pour the hot cream over the chocolate and let it sit undisturbed for 5 minutes. Whisk the mixture until it is smooth and creamy.

4. This recipe makes 1 cup of ganache. It can be stored in an airtight container in the refrigerator for up to 2 weeks.

WHIPPED CHOCOLATE GANACHE

Chocolate ganache is every chocolate lover's dream, but whipping it takes it to another level. Airy, fluffy, light - it's the ultimate indulgence!

INGREDIENTS

1 cup roughly chopped chocolate
1 cup heavy cream or whipping cream

METHOD

1. Put the chocolate in a heatproof bowl.

2. Heat the fresh cream in a saucepan until it begins to simmer.

3. Pour the hot cream over the chocolate and let it sit undisturbed for 5 minutes. Whisk the mixture until it is smooth and creamy. Transfer the ganache to the refrigerator and let it cool down for 1 hour.

4. Whip the cooled ganache using a hand mixer until it is light and fluffy.

5. This recipe makes 1 cup of whipped ganache. It can be stored in the refrigerator in an airtight container for up to 2 weeks, but make sure to whip it before using.

MERINGUE FROSTING

There's something magical about whipping up egg whites into a beautiful, shiny and smooth meringue. It's almost therapeutic to watch them double in size. And the best part? Using your blowtorch to give the frosting its beautiful golden brown colour.

INGREDIENTS

4 egg whites

2 cups caster sugar

¼ cup cold water

METHOD

1. Combine the egg whites, sugar and water in a heatproof bowl and place it over a saucepan of simmering water. Make sure the water does not touch the bottom of the bowl.

2. Using an electric hand mixer, whisk this mixture for 15 minutes, or until stiff peaks form. Take the bowl off the heat and let the meringue cool.

3. Use the frosting as soon as you make it. This frosting cannot be stored.

WHIPPED SALTED CARAMEL GANACHE

This salted caramel ganache is decadent and smooth. If you want to try something other than the simple chocolate ganache, then this one is for you!

INGREDIENTS

1 cup roughly chopped milk chocolate
1 cup granulated sugar
½ cup butter, softened
1 teaspoon sea salt
2 cups heavy cream

METHOD

1. Put the chocolate in a heatproof bowl and set aside.

2. Heat the sugar in a saucepan set over medium heat until it turns golden brown. Add the butter and sea salt and mix well till the butter has melted. Add the heavy cream. Stir continuously as it will bubble up vigorously.

3. Pour the hot caramel over the roughly chopped chocolate. Let the mixture sit undisturbed for 10 minutes. Whisk the caramel and chocolate together until combined.

4. Keep the salted caramel ganache in the refrigerator for 2 hours. If you do not intend to use the ganache immediately, you can store it in an airtight container in the refrigerator for up to 10 days, without whipping it.

5. When you are ready to use it, take the cold ganache out of the refrigerator and whip it using a stand mixer or a hand mixer on high speed until fluffy and light.

6. This recipe makes 2 cups of whipped ganache.

CHOCOLATE CREAM CHEESE FROSTING

This chocolate cream cheese frosting is for everyone who is all about chocolate, but wants to experiment a little with flavours. It's rich, creamy, and an absolute delight to whip up!

INGREDIENTS

2 cups icing sugar

½ cup cocoa powder

1 cup cream cheese, softened

½ cup butter, softened

METHOD

1. In a bowl, sift the icing sugar and cocoa powder together. Set aside.

2. In a large bowl, beat the cream cheese and butter until the mixture is light and fluffy. With the mixer still running, add the icing sugar and cocoa powder mixture in batches. Whisk until the frosting is smooth and fluffy.

3. This recipe makes 1 cup of frosting. It can be stored in an airtight container in the refrigerator for 3–4 days.

BLUEBERRY COMPOTE

This quick and simple blueberry compote is the
perfect topping for your pancakes, waffles, cakes and even ice creams.

INGREDIENTS

3 teaspoons cornflour

6 tablespoons water

1 cup frozen blueberries

½ cup sugar

METHOD

1. In a small bowl, dissolve the cornflour in water to make a paste. Set aside.

2. In a saucepan set over medium heat, cook the frozen blueberries with the sugar until they become slightly tender. Add the cornflour paste to the blueberries and let the mixture come to a boil and thicken. This may take a few minutes.

3. Take the compote off the heat and allow it to cool before using.

4. This recipe makes 1 cup of compote. It can be stored in an airtight container in the refrigerator for up to 10 days.

CHARCOAL CREAM CHEESE FROSTING

A creamy and smooth cream cheese frosting is great on its own, but when you want to make something unique, a charcoal cream cheese frosting is the way to go!

INGREDIENTS

1 cup cream cheese, softened
½ cup butter, softened
Beans from half a vanilla pod, or 1 teaspoon vanilla extract
1½ cups icing sugar, sifted
2 tablespoons activated charcoal

METHOD

1. In a bowl, beat the cream cheese with the butter until it is light and fluffy. Add the vanilla beans.

2. With the mixer still running, add the icing sugar in batches. It is necessary to sift the icing sugar as it may contain lumps. Beat the frosting until it is smooth and fluffy. Add the activated charcoal for colour.

3. This recipe makes 1 cup of frosting. It can stored in an airtight container in the refrigerator for 3–4 days.

VANILLA BUTTERCREAM FROSTING

Basic. Essential. Delicious. That's all I have to say about vanilla buttercream frosting. Every baker should have a vanilla buttercream frosting recipe up their sleeve and this one's mine.

INGREDIENTS

½ cup butter, softened
1 cup icing sugar, sifted
Beans from a vanilla pod
1–2 teaspoons milk

METHOD

1. In a bowl, beat the butter until it is completely smooth. With the mixer still running, gradually add the icing sugar. Sifting the icing sugar is important to remove any lumps.

2. Beat the frosting until it is light and fluffy. Mix in the vanilla beans. If the frosting is too dense, add a little milk and beat again until you get the desired consistency.

3. This recipe makes 1 cup of frosting. It can be stored in an airtight container in the refrigerator for 5–7 days.

LEMON CURD

One of my absolute favourite things to make is lemon curd. It's a staple in my kitchen and it goes on as many desserts as possible! This is a must-have recipe for every baker out there.

INGREDIENTS

2 eggs

¼ cup sugar

4 tablespoons fresh lemon juice

2 tablespoons butter

Zest of 1 lemon

½ tablespoon lemon essence

½ teaspoon vanilla extract

2–3 drops yellow food colouring (optional)

METHOD

1. In a saucepan set over medium heat, whisk together the eggs, sugar and lemon juice. Stir continuously to prevent curdling. Cook the mixture until it becomes thick and covers the back of your spoon. This will take approximately 10 minutes.

2. Take the saucepan off the heat, and add the butter to the hot mixture. Mix until the butter melts and is well incorporated.

3. Add the lemon zest, lemon essence, vanilla extract and the food colour. Mix well. Cover the mixture and let it cool in the refrigerator.

4. This recipe makes 1 cup of lemon curd. It can be stored in an airtight container in the refrigerator for 4–5 days.

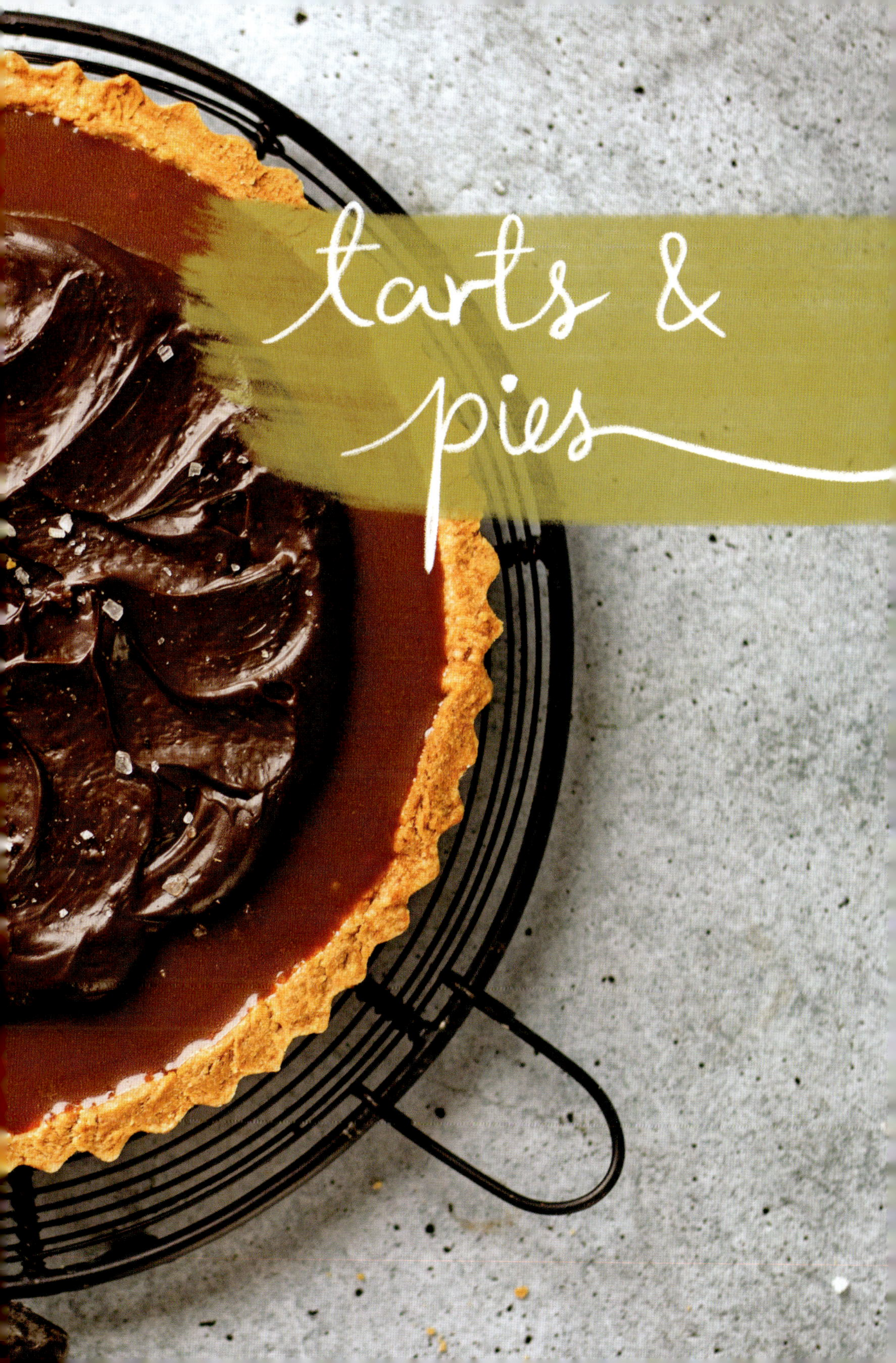
tarts &
pies

PLUM TART

A buttery, old-fashioned tart topped with sliced, juicy plums – this is one of the most beautiful desserts in this book, and is extremely simple to make. Serve it warm with some vanilla ice cream for the wow effect!

INGREDIENTS

For the tart shell

½ cup butter
¼ cup caster sugar
1 egg
1 teaspoon vanilla extract
1½ cups all-purpose flour

For the filling

8–9 plums, sliced
2 tablespoons butter, melted
1 tablespoon honey

METHOD

1. To make the tart shell, beat the butter and sugar in a bowl until light and fluffy. Whisk in the egg and vanilla extract. Add the flour and mix until the dough comes together.

2. Transfer the dough to a 9-inch tart pan with a removable bottom and press it into the bottom and the sides of the pan in an even layer using your fingers. Prick all over the base of the tart shell with a fork. Refrigerate the tart shell for at least 30 minutes.

3. Preheat the oven to 180°C.

4. Arrange the plum slices in the tart shell.

5. In a small bowl, combine the melted butter and honey to make a glaze. Generously brush this glaze on top of the plums.

6. Bake the tart for 20–25 minutes, or until golden brown. Serve warm.

LEMON TARTS

Growing up, lemon tarts were one of my most favourite desserts. And they still are.
So much so, that I felt I had to come up with an eggless version for *everyone* to enjoy!

INGREDIENTS

For the tart shell

½ cup butter

½ cup caster sugar

1¼ cups all-purpose flour

1 teaspoon vanilla

4 tablespoons milk

For the filling

1½ cups milk

2 tablespoons cornflour

2 teaspoons agar-agar powder

1 teaspoon vanilla extract

¾ cup lemon juice

½ cup honey or maple syrup

1 teaspoon lemon zest

For the topping

Fresh raspberries

METHOD

1. To make the tart shell, beat the butter and sugar in a large bowl. Add the flour and mix until well combined. Mix in the vanilla extract and milk. The dough will begin to come together.

2. Cover the dough with plastic wrap and chill for 30 minutes in the refrigerator.

3. To make the filling, bring the milk to a boil in a saucepan set over medium heat. Whisk in the cornflour, agar-agar powder and vanilla extract. Continue to cook until the mixture begins to thicken. Add the lemon juice and honey (or maple syrup), whisking constantly.

4. Take the mixture off the heat and strain it into a heatproof bowl. Mix in the lemon zest. Let the filling cool completely.

5. Preheat the oven to 180°C.

6. Roll the tart dough on a lightly floured surface till it is about 3 mm thick. Transfer the rolled-out dough into a 9-inch tart pan or cut smaller circles for five 3-inch tart rings. Use a fork to prick all over the tart shell.

7. Bake the tart shells for about 15–20 minutes until golden brown. Cool them on a wire rack and unmould them carefully.

8. Pour the lemon filling into the tart shells and refrigerate them for 3–4 hours to allow the filling to set. Top with the fresh raspberries.

APPLE RASPBERRY PIE

I avoided making pies for the longest time simply because they looked so scary to put together. Pies can be intimidating but, just once, let go of your fear and you'll see the magic unfold. Remember, the dough can sense your fear. Treat it with love!

INGREDIENTS

For the crust

1¼ cups all-purpose flour
2 tablespoons granulated sugar
⅓ cup unsalted cold butter, cubed
1–2 tablespoons cold water

For the filling

3 apples, diced, peel on
¾ cup frozen raspberries
½ cup caster sugar
2 tablespoons lemon juice
2 tablespoons cornflour

For the topping

A splash of milk
2 tablespoons caster sugar, to top the unbaked pie

METHOD

1. To make the crust, pulse the flour, granulated sugar and butter in a food processor until it resembles a coarse meal. Add water and mix until the dough comes together. Divide the dough into two halves and wrap each half in plastic wrap. Let the dough chill in the refrigerator for at least 1 hour before you begin rolling it out.

2. To make the filling, combine the apples, raspberries, sugar, lemon juice and cornflour in a large bowl. Set aside.

3. Preheat the oven to 180°C.

4. Dust a clean surface lightly with flour. Roll out one half of the dough into a circle, ⅛ inch thick. Once rolled to the desired size, lightly wrap the pie crust around a rolling pin and unroll it on top of the pie pan (7–8 inches in diameter). Gently press it into the bottom and sides of the pie dish. Trim the dough along the edge of the dish. If the dough feels too soft, let it rest in the refrigerator for longer. If the pie dough cracks while working, roll it out again or simply use a wet finger to fix the crack. Pour the filling into the crust.

5. Roll out the other half of the dough into a circle, ⅛ inch thick. Using a knife, cut it into long strips. Carefully lift and place these on top of the filling, pressing one end into the edge of the pie. Alternate the strips to create a lattice on top. Secure the other end of the strip as well.

6. Brush the crust with milk and sprinkle the caster sugar on top. Bake the pie for 1 hour, until it turns golden brown.

CRÈME BRÛLÉE TARTS

Loosely translated, crème brûlée means burnt cream. With its soft, creamy custard
and crunchy topping, I know these orange–hazelnut crème brûlée tarts will
blow your mind.

INGREDIENTS

For the tart shell

½ cup butter

½ cup caster sugar

1 egg yolk

1 cup all-purpose flour

¼ cup ground hazelnuts

For the filling

2 cups heavy cream

1 tablespoon orange zest

1 teaspoon vanilla extract

3 egg yolks

½ cup caster sugar

For the topping

¼ cup caster sugar

METHOD

1. To make the tart shell, beat together the butter and sugar in a large bowl. Whisk in the egg yolk. Fold in the flour and ground hazelnuts and mix until the dough comes together.

2. Press the dough into the bottom and along the sides of four 3-inch round tart rings. Keep the tart shells in the refrigerator to chill for 2 hours.

3. To make the filling, combine the heavy cream, orange zest and vanilla extract in a saucepan over medium heat. Allow the mixture to come to a simmer, then take it off the heat.

4. Meanwhile, in a bowl, whisk together the egg yolks and sugar till pale and light. Gradually pour the hot cream into the egg mixture, continuously whisking to ensure there are no lumps. Strain this filling and set aside to cool.

5. Preheat the oven to 180°C. Partially bake the chilled tart shells for 7–8 minutes.

6. Reduce the temperature to 150°C. Pour the cooled filling into the tart shells and bake for 18–22 minutes, or until almost set. Remove the tarts from the oven and let them cool completely.

7. Before serving, sprinkle a tablespoon of caster sugar evenly over the filling and use a kitchen torch to brûlée it. If you don't have a blowtorch, heat up the convex side of a big metal spoon over a flame. Once it becomes extremely hot, press it down on the sugar.

CARAMEL CHOCOLATE TART

I really struggled to get this recipe right – either the caramel was too runny or the tart shell was too weak – until finally, everything clicked into place! Here's the best version we made. I know you'll love it too!

INGREDIENTS

For the tart shell

½ cup butter
4 tablespoons caster sugar
1¼ cups all-purpose flour

For the filling

2 cups granulated sugar
1 cup butter
1 cup heavy cream
2 tablespoons corn syrup

For the topping

1 cup chocolate ganache
(see p. 140)
A pinch of sea salt

METHOD

1. To make the tart shell, beat the butter and sugar together with a whisk or spatula. Fold in the flour and mix until the dough begins to come together. Using your fingers, press the dough into the bottom and the sides of 9-inch tart pan with a removable bottom in an even layer. Refrigerate the shell for at least 30 minutes.

2. Preheat the oven to 180°C.

3. Once the tart shell has chilled, using a fork, prick the base of the tart shell. Bake for 10–15 minutes, or until the tart shell is golden brown. Let it cool completely, then carefully remove it from the tart pan.

4. To make the filling, cook the sugar in a saucepan over medium heat until it turns amber in colour. Mix in the butter until it emulsifies completely into the sugar. Take the caramel off the heat and add the cream, stirring continuously. The mixture will bubble up furiously, so be careful. Return the saucepan to the heat and add the corn syrup. Cook the caramel for 5 minutes over a medium-low flame till it begins to boil.

5. Let the caramel cool in the refrigerator for 30 minutes before pouring it into the tart shell. Place the tart in the refrigerator overnight and let it set.

6. Spread the chocolate ganache on top and sprinkle some sea salt before serving.

MANGO LIME PUFF PASTRY TARTS

The combination of fresh mango, creamy mascarpone and zingy lime in buttery puff pastry makes this dessert irresistible. One bite and you're transported to flavour heaven!

INGREDIENTS

Store-bought puff pastry dough
½ cup mascarpone cheese
⅓ cup icing sugar
Zest of 2 limes
1 mango, peeled and thinly sliced
A splash of milk

METHOD

1. Preheat the oven to 180°C. Line a baking tray with parchment paper or a silicon mat.

2. Roll out the puff pastry dough on a lightly floured surface and cut out three 4-inch circles.

3. Using a knife, score the pastry, leaving a 1-inch border from the edge. Be careful that you don't cut through to the bottom.

4. In a bowl, cream the mascarpone cheese until fluffy, then add the icing sugar and lime zest and mix well. Spread this filling inside the circles using an offset spatula.

5. Arrange the thinly sliced mango on top of the filling.

6. Transfer the puff pastry tarts to the lined baking tray and brush the borders with milk.

7. Bake for 15–20 minutes, until the pastry has puffed up and turned golden brown.

STRAWBERRY BRIOCHE TART

Rich buttery pastry with a generous layer of almond cream and some fresh strawberries baked to perfection – is there anything better?

INGREDIENTS

For the brioche

1 teaspoon caster sugar

¼ cup warm water

½ tablespoon active dry yeast

1¾ cups all-purpose flour

½ teaspoon salt

2 eggs

½ cup butter

1 egg yolk mixed with
1 teaspoon cold milk for the egg wash

1 tablespoon sesame seeds, to top

For the almond cream

½ cup almond flour

½ tablespoon all-purpose flour

Zest of 1 orange

¼ cup butter

¼ cup powdered sugar

1 egg

1 teaspoon vanilla extract

For the topping

Fresh strawberries

METHOD

1. To make the brioche, in a small bowl, dissolve the sugar in warm water and add the active dry yeast to the solution. Let it sit for 10 minutes until it foams up and appears milky.

2. In a large bowl, combine the flour and salt. Make a well in the middle of the flour and pour in the yeast solution and add the eggs. Using an electric mixer, mix on low speed until a dough forms, occasionally scraping the sides of the bowl. With the mixer still running, gradually add the butter in small quantities. Allow each addition of butter to mix in before adding the next. Once all the butter has been added, knead the dough in the mixer for 5–8 minutes. The dough will be very sticky at this point. Transfer the dough into a clean, greased bowl. Cover it with plastic wrap and let it rest for 1 hour, or until it doubles up in volume, at room temperature. Refrigerate the dough for at least 12 hours, up to a day.

3. Roll out the chilled dough into a 9-inch circle, about ¼-inch thick. Place it on a baking tray lined with parchment paper and allow the dough to proof at room temperature for 90 minutes.

4. Preheat the oven to 180°C, 15 minutes before the brioche is done proofing.

5. To make the almond cream, combine the almond flour, all-purpose flour and orange zest in a bowl and set aside.

6. In another bowl, beat together the butter and sugar until light and fluffy. Add in the egg and vanilla, and mix well. Fold the dry ingredients into this mixture.

7. Apply a thick layer of this almond cream onto the proofed brioche dough, leaving a ½-inch border all around.

8. Brush the border of the pastry with the egg wash and sprinkle sesame seeds on it.

9. Top the almond cream generously with fresh strawberries.

10. Bake the brioche tart for 45 minutes.

CHERRY HAND PIES

A dessert with a flaky crust, juicy filling and just the right amount of nostalgia –
what says summer more than a cherry pie?

INGREDIENTS

For the pie crust

1¼ cups all-purpose flour

2 tablespoons caster sugar

⅓ cup cold butter, cubed

1–2 tablespoons cold water

A splash of milk

2 tablespoons caster sugar,
to top the unbaked pies

For the filling

½ cup pitted cherries

4 tablespoons caster sugar

1½ tablespoons cornflour

1 tablespoon lemon juice

METHOD

1. To make the pie crust, pulse the flour, sugar and butter in a food processor until it resembles a coarse meal. Add the water and pulse until the dough comes together. Divide the dough into two halves and wrap each half separately in plastic wrap. Let the dough chill in the refrigerator for at least 1 hour before you begin rolling it out.

2. To make the filling, combine the cherries, sugar, cornflour and lemon juice in a large bowl and set aside.

3. Preheat the oven to 180°C. Line a baking tray with parchment paper and set aside.

4. Lightly dust a clean surface with flour. Roll out one half of the dough into a circle, ⅛ inch thick. Cut out 3-inch-wide circles from the dough and transfer them to the baking tray. Spoon some of the cherry filling into the centre of each circle, leaving a ½-inch border around the edge.

5. Roll out the other half of the dough and cut out 3-inch-wide circles. With a smaller cutter, cut out the centre. Place the circles on top of the cherry filling and then crimp the edges with a fork.

6. Brush the pies with egg wash and sprinkle caster sugar on top.

7. Bake the pies for 20–25 minutes until they turn golden brown.

BANOFFEE PIE

Decadence and deliciousness – these are the hallmarks of a banoffee pie. It's incredibly easy to whip up. And it brings together the ultimate duo of caramel and bananas. Need I say more? Once you make this pie, you'll be hooked!

INGREDIENTS

For the crust

2 cups digestive biscuits, crushed
1 cup butter, melted

For the filling

1 can condensed milk
2 bananas, sliced
1 cup whipped cream
Chocolate shavings, to top

METHOD

1. To make the crust, combine the crushed biscuits and melted butter. The mixture will have the consistency of wet sand. Press the biscuit mixture into two 4.5-inch or one 9-inch tart pan in an even layer. Refrigerate for 1 hour to set.

2. To make the dulce de leche filling, place the can of condensed milk in a large pot. Fill the pot with water until the can is completely submerged. Cover the pot and place it over heat. Allow it to simmer for 2–3 hours, depending on how dark you want the dulce de leche to be. Make sure the can is completely submerged in boiling water throughout. Add more boiling water when required. Allow the can to cool completely before opening. Fill the chilled tart shell with the caramelized condensed milk.

3. Refrigerate for at least 2 hours.

4. Arrange sliced bananas on the cooled tart, and top generously with whipped cream and chocolate shavings.

PEACH FRANGIPANE TART

I dream about the frangipane tart I had in San Francisco's Tartine Bakery a few years ago. So I decided to create one of my own and share this decadent dessert with all of you! The almond cream combined with fresh peaches makes this as dreamy a dessert as can be.

INGREDIENTS

For the tart shell

½ cup butter
½ cup caster sugar
¼ cup light brown sugar, packed
1 egg yolk
1 cup oat flour
¼ cup rolled oats

For the filling

4 tablespoons butter
½ cup caster sugar
1 cup ground almonds
2 eggs
2½ tablespoons oat flour
Zest of 1 orange
7–10 peaches, sliced thinly
Flaked almonds, to top

METHOD

1. Preheat the oven to 180°C.

2. To make the tart shell, beat together the butter, caster sugar and light brown sugar in a large bowl. Mix in the egg yolk. Fold in the oat flour and rolled oats and mix until the dough comes together.

3. Press the dough into the bottom and sides of a 14x4.5-inch rectangular tart pan. Using a fork, prick the tart shell all over.

4. Bake for 10–15 minutes, or until the shell is slightly golden in colour.

5. To make the filling, in a large bowl, beat the butter and sugar until pale and fluffy. Add the ground almonds and mix to combine. Whisk in the eggs, one at a time, beating well after each addition. Add the oat flour and orange zest, and combine well. Pour the filling into the prepared tart shell.

6. Place the peach slices and scatter the flaked almonds on top.

7. Bake the tart for another 20–25 minutes, or until it is golden brown.

CHERRY PUFF PASTRY TART

I love how versatile puff pastry dough is! The juiciness of cherries
and the texture of the puff pastry crust come together to make
a perfect combination.

INGREDIENTS

Store-bought puff pastry
½ cup almond cream
(see p. 173)
1 cup pitted cherries
¼ cup flaked almonds
A splash of milk

METHOD

1. Preheat the oven to 180°C. Line a baking tray
   with parchment paper and set aside.

2. On a lightly floured surface, roll out the puff pastry
   into a 6-inch circle. Using a knife, score the circle,
   1 inch from the edge. Make sure the knife doesn't
   go through and through.

3. Spread the almond cream inside the border using
   an offset spatula. Arrange the cherries and almond
   flakes over the cream, leaving the border empty.
   Brush the edges of the puff pastry with the milk.

4. Bake for 15–20 minutes, or until the edge is
   golden brown.

VEGAN VANILLA TART

My sisters have been vegan for many years and this tart by far is one of their favourite desserts. One of the challenges of vegan baking is the non-availability of ingredients that recipes typically call for. That is one problem I seek to solve with recipes like this one.

INGREDIENTS

For the tart shell

1 cup all-purpose flour
½ cup ground almonds
⅔ cup coconut oil, cold
¼ cup cold water

For the filling

2 tablespoons vanilla extract
2 cups coconut cream
8 tablespoons maple syrup
4 tablespoons cornflour
3 teaspoons agar-agar powder

For the topping

Sliced peaches and plums

METHOD

1. To make the tart shell, combine the all-purpose flour and ground almonds in a bowl. Use your hands to mix in the cold coconut oil until the mixture resembles wet sand. Add the cold water and continue mixing until the dough comes together. Knead the dough into a ball. Cover it with plastic wrap and refrigerate for 10–15 minutes, or until the oil starts to harden.

2. Preheat the oven to 180°C.

3. Roll out the dough till it is ⅛ inch thick. Using the rolling pin, transfer it to a 9-inch round tart pan with a removable bottom. Prick the crust with a fork and bake for 15–20 minutes, or until the tart shell becomes golden brown. Set aside to cool.

4. To make the filling, whisk together the vanilla extract, coconut cream, maple syrup and cornflour in a small saucepan until no lumps remain. Set the saucepan over medium heat, and bring the mixture to a slow boil. Continue whisking as it thickens to avoid burning it. When the custard starts to boil, add the agar-agar, and mix well. Take the custard off the heat.

5. Pour the vanilla custard into the baked tart shell. Refrigerate the tart for at least 4 hours.

6. Once the filling has set, top it with the sliced peaches and plums.

CHOCOLATE TART WITH VANILLA CUSTARD AND RASPBERRIES

Chocolate and vanilla is a classic combination. I added raspberries in the mix to take things up a notch! Try it and see for yourself.

INGREDIENTS

For the tart shell

½ cup butter

¼ cup caster sugar

1 egg, lightly beaten

1 cup all-purpose flour

½ cup cocoa powder

For the filling

1½ cups heavy cream

½ cup all-purpose flour

1 cup caster sugar

4 large eggs

2 teaspoons vanilla extract

1 cup fresh raspberries

METHOD

1. To make the tart shell, beat the butter and sugar in a bowl until light and fluffy. Whisk in the egg. Add the flour and cocoa powder and mix until completely combined. Cover the dough in plastic wrap and chill for about 1 hour.

2. Preheat the oven to 180°C.

3. Using your fingers, press the chilled dough into the bottom and sides of a 9-inch tart pan with a removable bottom in an even layer and bake it for 10 minutes. Set aside.

4. To make the filling, warm the heavy cream in a small saucepan over low heat.

5. Meanwhile, in a large bowl mix the flour and sugar together. Whisk in the eggs and stir with a wooden spoon to make a smooth paste. Do not let this mixture sit for too long as it will form a crust.

6. Once the cream begins to simmer, take it off the heat and gradually whisk it into the egg mixture, stirring constantly. Add the vanilla extract.

7. Pour the filling into the prepared tart shell and top it with fresh raspberries.

8. Bake the tart for 20–25 minutes, or until it becomes light golden on top and the custard is firm.

BROWNIE PECAN TART

Chocolate and pecan is a match made in baker's heaven! What's better than brownies?
A pecan brownie in a chocolatey tart shell!

INGREDIENTS

For the tart shell

½ cup butter

¼ cup caster sugar

1 egg

1 teaspoon vanilla extract

1 cup all-purpose flour

½ cup cocoa powder

For the filling

1 cup dark chocolate,
coarsely chopped

½ cup butter

1 cup caster sugar

2 eggs

½ cup all-purpose flour

3 tablespoons cocoa powder

1 teaspoon baking powder

1 cup pecans

METHOD

1. To make the tart shell, beat the butter and sugar in a bowl until light and fluffy. Whisk in the egg and vanilla extract. Add the flour and cocoa powder and mix until the dough comes together.

2. Transfer the dough to a 9-inch tart pan with a removable bottom. Use your fingers to press the dough into the bottom and the sides of the pan in an even layer. Refrigerate the shell for at least 30 minutes.

3. Preheat the oven to 180°C.

4. To make the brownie filling, melt the chocolate and butter in a saucepan set over low heat. Let the mixture cool.

5. In a bowl, whisk together the sugar and eggs. Pour in the cooled chocolate mixture. Now add the flour, cocoa powder and baking powder and mix until just combined.

6. Pour this brownie filling into the tart shell and arrange the pecans over it.

7. Bake the tart for 25–30 minutes, or until the filling is set.

more sweet
treats

BANANA BREAD WITH CHOCOLATE CHUNKS

I think eggless desserts are interesting only if they taste as good as the version that uses eggs. But, guess what! This eggless banana bread is even better than the one with eggs! When I need a slice of comfort with my coffee, this is the recipe I turn to.

INGREDIENTS

2 cups all-purpose flour

1 teaspoon baking powder

½ teaspoon baking soda

¼ teaspoon instant coffee powder

½ cup butter

¼ cup caster sugar

2 teaspoons vanilla extract

1½ cup mashed ripe bananas

½ cup milk

1 cup chocolate chunks

½ cup chopped walnuts

Banana slices, to top

Chocolate chunks, to top

METHOD

1. Preheat the oven to 180°C. Line a 9x4-inch loaf pan with parchment paper.

2. In a large bowl, whisk together the flour, baking powder, baking soda and coffee powder.

3. In another bowl, cream the butter and sugar until the mixture is pale and fluffy. Add the vanilla extract and the bananas, making sure everything is well incorporated. Whisk in the milk.

4. Fold the dry ingredients into the wet ingredients until just combined. Add the chocolate chunks and chopped walnuts. The batter will be thick.

5. Transfer the batter into the prepared loaf pan and top with sliced bananas and chocolate chunks.

6. Bake the loaf for 40–50 minutes. Let it cool a little before slicing and serving.

GINGER PANNA COTTA WITH SPICED PLUM COMPOTE

There aren't too many things that make me as happy as a beautifully set panna cotta sliding out of the mould and landing on the plate with a little wobble.

INGREDIENTS

For the plum compote

6 ripe red plums, pitted and sliced

2 tablespoons light brown sugar

1 cinnamon stick

4 tablespoons water

For the panna cotta

3 gelatin leaves, or 1 tablespoon gelatin powder, soaked in 6 tablespoons cold water, left undisturbed for 5–10 minutes

1 cup whole milk

1 cup double cream

1 teaspoon pure vanilla extract, or beans of 1 vanilla pod

2 tablespoons granulated sugar

3 tablespoons ginger powder

METHOD

1. To make the compote, combine the plums, brown sugar and cinnamon stick and water in a non-stick saucepan over medium heat. Stir well to dissolve the sugar. Bring the mixture to a simmer. Cover the pan and allow it to cook for 5–10 minutes or until the plums have softened, stirring occasionally. Take the mixture off the heat and let it cool a little. Remove the cinnamon stick and refrigerate the compote.

2. To make the panna cotta, mix the milk, cream, vanilla extract, sugar and ginger powder in a saucepan set over medium heat, and bring the mixture to a simmer. Take the pan off the heat.

3. Squeeze the water out of the soaked gelatin leaves and add them to the cream mixture while it is still warm. Stir until the gelatin has dissolved.

4. Pour the mixture into ramekins or any other lightly greased glass/ceramic ware and refrigerate overnight.

5. Unmould the panna cotta and serve with the spiced plum compote.

WHOLEWHEAT PANCAKES

Bring out those bowls and the whisk and throw a breakfast party.
Don't forget to send my invite!

INGREDIENTS

½ cup wholewheat flour

1 teaspoon baking powder

½ teaspoon cinnamon powder

A pinch of salt

2 tablespoons caster sugar

½ cup milk mixed with 1 teaspoon vinegar, rested for 5 minutes

3 tablespoons vegetable oil, plus extra for brushing the pan

½ teaspoon vanilla extract

METHOD

1. In a bowl, mix the flour, baking powder, cinnamon powder, salt and sugar. Gradually whisk in the milk, vegetable oil and vanilla extract. Combine the ingredients thoroughly and make sure there are no lumps. The consistency of your batter should be pourable but quite thick to ensure the pancakes have a good texture. You may need to add some more milk to get the desired consistency.

2. Let the batter rest for 10–15 minutes to allow the baking powder to react with the other ingredients, which will result in soft and fluffy pancakes.

3. Brush a non-stick pan with vegetable oil and set it over medium heat. Ladle about ¼ cup of the batter into the pan for each pancake. Cook for about 2 minutes and gently flip. Cook on the other side for 1 minute. Repeat with the remaining batter. Serve the pancakes with your favourite toppings.

4. This recipe makes 8–10 pancakes.

CHOCOLATE WALNUT BROWNIES

This recipe is for anyone who has not been able to experience the bliss that comes with eating a chocolate walnut brownie because it has egg in it. Dark, fudgy and delightful – these brownies are a must-have!

INGREDIENTS

½ cup butter
1 cup dark chocolate, coarsely chopped
1 cup caster sugar
1 cup Greek yogurt
½ cup all-purpose flour
3 tablespoons cocoa powder
1 teaspoon baking powder
½ cup crushed walnuts

METHOD

1. Preheat the oven to 180°C. Butter an 8-inch square pan or line it with parchment paper.

2. Melt the butter and chocolate in a saucepan set over low heat. Let the mixture cool.

3. In a bowl, combine the sugar and Greek yogurt. Whisk in the cooled chocolate and butter mixture. Fold in the flour, cocoa powder and baking powder, mixing until everything is just combined. Add the walnuts.

4. Transfer the batter to the baking pan. Bake for 30–35 minutes. Let the brownies cool completely before you cut them. They can be stored in an airtight container for 3–4 days.

ROSE CHEESECAKE ICE CREAM

What do you do when you are craving a rich, creamy cheesecake, but the weather calls for ice cream? You make this perfectly balanced rose cheesecake ice cream!

INGREDIENTS

1 cup cream cheese, softened

1 cup caster sugar

2 cups heavy cream

1 cup milk

1½ teaspoon rose extract

3–4 drops pink food colouring

½ cup crushed
digestive biscuits

METHOD

1. In a large bowl, combine the cream cheese and sugar until smooth. Whisk in the heavy cream and milk. Make sure the mixture is smooth and there are no lumps. Add the rose extract and food colour.

2. Transfer this mixture to the bowl of an ice cream maker, and churn as per the manufacturer's directions.

3. Once the mixture has churned, fold in the crushed digestive biscuits and transfer to a loaf pan. Cover and freeze for at least 6 hours so the ice cream can set.

BUCKWHEAT NECTARINE GALETTE

This free-form galette is super easy and lots of fun to make. Warm flavourful fruit wrapped in a flaky gluten-free pastry served with a large scoop of vanilla ice cream – delicious!

INGREDIENTS

For the crust

1 cup buckwheat flour

¼ cup ground almonds

½ cup cold butter, cubed

4 tablespoons granulated sugar

4 tablespoons ice-cold water

A splash of milk

½ cup flaked almonds, to top

For the filling

8–10 nectarines, thinly sliced

5–6 blackberries

2 tablespoons fresh lemon juice

4 tablespoons honey

¼ cup ground almonds

METHOD

1. To make the crust, put the buckwheat flour, ground almonds, cold butter and sugar in a food processor and pulse until the mixture is coarse and crumbly. Add the cold water and pulse again until the mixture begins to hold together when pinched. Turn the mixture out onto a flat surface and bring it together. Shape the dough into a disc, wrap it in plastic wrap and refrigerate for 30 minutes.

2. To make the filling, toss the nectarines and blackberries in lemon juice and honey, and set aside.

3. Preheat the oven to 180°C.

4. On a piece of parchment paper, roll out the chilled dough into a circle, ⅛ inch thick. Leaving a 1-inch border around the edge, evenly spread the ground almonds on the rolled-out dough. Arrange the nectarine slices and blackberries on top of the ground almonds. Fold the edges of the dough over the fruit. Generously brush the overlapping dough with milk and top with the flaked almonds.

5. Carefully lift the parchment paper and transfer it onto a baking tray.

6. Bake for 40-45 minutes, or until the crust has cooked completely.

7. Let the galette cool on the baking tray before removing. Serve with vanilla ice cream.

CHOCOLATE AND FIG PUDDING

I had never imagined that the combination of fig and chocolate would turn out to be so good. This pudding is rich and delicious, just perfect for Christmas.

INGREDIENTS

1¼ cups dried figs, chopped

1 cup water

1 teaspoon baking soda

½ cup butter

½ cup light brown sugar

¼ cup honey

2 eggs

1½ cups all-purpose flour

2 teaspoons baking powder

1 teaspoon salt

1 cup chopped dark chocolate

1 cup toffee sauce, to serve (see p. 80)

METHOD

1. Preheat the oven to 180°C. Line a 7x11-inch pan with parchment paper.

2. Combine the dried figs, water and baking soda in a saucepan over medium heat. Bring the mixture to a boil and then reduce the heat and let it simmer for 2 minutes. Take the pan off the heat and let the fig mixture cool for a while. Once it has cooled, mash it with a spoon, breaking down the fruit to get a paste.

3. In a large bowl, beat the butter, sugar and honey together. Whisk in the eggs. Add the flour, baking powder and the salt, and mix until combined.

4. Melt the chopped dark chocolate in a heatproof bowl set over a pan of simmering water (or in the microwave in 30-second increments, stirring each time, to avoid burning the chocolate) until smooth.

5. Add the melted chocolate and the fig paste to the batter and mix thoroughly.

6. Transfer the batter into the prepared baking pan and bake for 30–35 minutes, or until it forms a crust on top.

7. Serve with toffee sauce.

POPCORN HONEYCOMB

Every month we make a big batch of honeycomb in our kitchen, and then decorate
our cakes with it and crumble it over our ice creams. The only problem is I don't know when
to stop eating it. It's a snaccident waiting to happen!

INGREDIENTS

1 cup popcorn, popped

1 cup caster sugar

6 tablespoons golden syrup

2 teaspoons baking soda

METHOD

1. Line a 10x6-inch baking tray with parchment paper.

2. Spread the popcorn evenly all over the tray.

3. In a saucepan set over medium heat, cook the caster sugar and golden syrup until the sugar melts. Continue cooking until the mixture turns amber in colour. Take it off the heat and add the baking soda immediately. The mixture will bubble up vigorously. Give it a stir and quickly pour it over the popcorn.

4. Let the honeycomb sit at room temperature for 30 minutes until it hardens. Remove it from the parchment paper and break into shards. Store the popcorn honeycomb in an airtight container.

STRAWBERRY GALETTE

Galette comes from the Norman word 'gale', meaning flat cake. This recipe is easy, delicious, and beautifully rustic. What's not to love!

INGREDIENTS

For the crust

1 cup wholewheat flour
¼ cup rolled oats
½ cup cold butter, cubed
4 tablespoons granulated sugar
4 tablespoons ice-cold water
A splash of milk

For the filling

8–10 strawberries, thinly sliced
¼ cup caster sugar
1 tablespoon lemon zest
¼ cup ground almonds

METHOD

1. To make the crust, combine the wholewheat flour, rolled oats, cold butter and sugar in a food processor, until the mixture resembles coarse sand. Add the cold water and pulse until the mixture begins to hold together when pinched. Turn out the dough onto a flat surface and bring it together; do not overwork it. Shape the dough into a disc, cover it with plastic wrap and refrigerate it for 30 minutes.

2. To make the filling, combine the strawberries, caster sugar and lemon zest in a bowl, and set aside.

3. Preheat the oven to 180°C.

4. On a piece of parchment paper, roll out the dough into a circle, about ¼ inch thick. Leaving a 1-inch border around the edge, evenly spread the ground almonds over the rolled-out dough. Arrange the strawberry slices over the ground almonds. Fold the edges of the crust over the fruit. Generously brush the folded dough with the milk.

5. Carefully lift the parchment paper and transfer it onto a baking tray.

6. Bake for 20–30 minutes, or until the crust is golden brown.

7. Let the galette cool on the baking tray completely before removing it. Serve with ice cream.

LITCHI ROSE TIRAMISU

Doesn't just the name of this dessert conjure up images of romance and decadence?
Tiramisu is one of my all-time favourite desserts. This version of the classic is sure to
be the showstopper at your next gathering. Save this recipe!

INGREDIENTS

½ cup water

¼ cup rose water

4 tablespoons caster sugar

1 cup fresh litchi puree

½ cup mascarpone cheese

4 tablespoons icing sugar

½ cup heavy cream, chilled

10–15 ladyfinger biscuits

½ cup fresh raspberries

10–12 fresh litchis

METHOD

1. In a saucepan set over medium heat, bring the water, rose water and caster sugar to a boil. Let the sugar dissolve completely. Set the syrup aside to cool.

2. In a bowl, combine the litchi puree, mascarpone cheese and icing sugar, and set aside.

3. In another bowl, beat the heavy cream using an electric mixture on high speed until it doubles in volume and forms soft peaks.

4. Gently fold the litchi puree and mascarpone mix into the whipped cream using a spatula. Transfer the filling into a piping bag.

5. To assemble the tiramisu, dip the ladyfinger biscuits into the rose water syrup and layer them in a dessert glass or a shallow dish. Do not soak them or let them sit in the syrup for too long. Pipe the filling over the biscuits. Top with fresh litchis and raspberries. Repeat to form layers.

6. Let the tiramisu set in the refrigerator for 30–40 minutes before serving.

PEACH AND BLUEBERRY CRISPS

Peach and blueberry is one of my favourite go-to flavour combinations. The tartness of the blueberries complements the sweet peaches beautifully in this recipe.

INGREDIENTS

For the filling

3–4 peaches, sliced
½ cup frozen blueberries
¼ cup light brown sugar
2 tablespoons cornflour
1 tablespoon fresh
lemon juice

For the topping

1½ cups rolled oats
1 cup wholewheat flour
½ cup light brown sugar
¼ cup cold butter, cubed
1 teaspoon vanilla extract

METHOD

1. Preheat the oven to 180°C.

2. To make the fruit filling, in a large bowl, toss the peach slices and blueberries with the sugar, cornflour and lemon juice. Set aside.

3. To make the crisp topping, combine the oats, flour and sugar in a bowl. Add the butter and vanilla extract and mix until everything is combined and you get a coarse mixture.

4. Transfer the fruit filling into glass ramekins and scatter the crisp topping evenly over the mixture, leaving the large clumps intact.

5. Bake for 30–35 minutes, until the fruit juices are bubbling around the edges and the topping turns golden brown.

MANGO PASSION FRUIT PAVLOVA

When you're making this pavlova, don't forget to hold the mixing bowl upside down over your friend's head to see if the egg whites are stiff enough!

INGREDIENTS

For the pavlova

4 egg whites
2 cups caster sugar
2 tablespoons cornflour
1 teaspoon vanilla extract

For the topping

1 teaspoon lime zest
½ cup whipped cream
1 mango, sliced
¼ cup raspberries
¼ cup passion fruit puree

METHOD

1. Preheat the oven to 100°C. Draw a 6-inch circle on a piece of parchment paper and place it upside down on a baking tray.

2. To make the pavlova, take the egg whites in a clean bowl. Make sure the bowl does not have any water or grease. With an electric mixer, beat the egg whites at high speed until they double in volume. With the mixer still running, add the sugar, 1 tablespoon at a time, followed by the cornflour and vanilla extract. Keep mixing at high speed until the meringue becomes glossy and forms stiff peaks. Spread it on the parchment paper, making sure you stay inside the circle. Bake for 1 hour.

3. While the pavlova is baking, fold the lime zest into the whipped cream.

4. To assemble the pavlova, top it with the whipped cream, mango slices and raspberries. Drizzle the passion fruit puree on top. Serve immediately.

BERLINERS

If you're a fan of doughnuts, you're going to love making Berliners. These are a traditional Austrian pastry that are usually filled with jam and covered in icing sugar. It took six attempts to get these right but watching these little dough balls puff up was well worth the effort!

INGREDIENTS

For the dough

2 tablespoons caster sugar

2 tablespoons lukewarm water

2¼ teaspoons active dry yeast

1½ cup all-purpose flour

2 eggs

2 tablespoons butter

½ cup caster sugar mixed with 2 teaspoons cinnamon powder

For the pastry cream

1¼ cups milk

3 egg yolks

¼ cup caster sugar

2 tablespoons all-purpose flour

2 tablespoons cornflour

2 teaspoons vanilla extract

4 tablespoons butter

METHOD

1. To make the dough, mix 1 tablespoon of caster sugar in a bowl with the lukewarm water and add the yeast to it. Let the mixture sit for 10 minutes until it is bubbly.

2. In a large bowl, whisk together the flour, the remaining 1 tablespoon sugar and the eggs. Add the yeast mixture and combine. Knead the dough for 10–15 minutes. Once the dough is smooth and elastic, add the butter and knead until it has been absorbed. Cover and rest the dough for 2 hours, or until it doubles up in volume. Make equal-sized portions of the dough and seal them to make perfect dough balls. Allow them to proof for another 3–4 hours outside or overnight in the refrigerator. Once proofed, fry the Berliners until they're golden on both sides. Immediately roll the hot Berliners in the cinnamon sugar.

3. To make pastry cream, bring the milk to a boil in a saucepan set over medium heat.

4. In a bowl, combine the egg yolks, sugar, flour and cornflour. Mix well to obtain a smooth paste. Gradually pour the boiled milk into the paste, stirring constantly to prevent curdling. Pour the mixture back into the saucepan and cook over low heat, whisking constantly, to thicken the pastry cream. Once the cream has thickened, remove it from the heat. Add the vanilla extract and butter and mix well. Let it cool. Transfer the pastry cream into a piping bag with a round piping tip.

5. Make a small incision in the Berliners and fill them until the pastry cream oozes out.

S'MORES

S'mores are a classic sweet treat famous all around the world. I could munch on them all day long. The combination of gooey toasted marshmallows, warm chocolate and crispy graham crackers is irresistible.

INGREDIENTS

1 cup wholewheat flour

½ cup all-purpose flour

⅓ cup caster sugar

¼ teaspoon baking powder

¼ teaspoon baking soda

½ cup butter, cubed and chilled

1 tablespoon honey

2 tablespoons milk

½ teaspoon vanilla extract

1 cup chocolate ganache (see p. 140)

1 cup marshmallows

METHOD

1. In a bowl, whisk together the wholewheat flour, all-purpose flour, sugar, baking powder and baking soda. Mix the cold butter into the flour mixture until it develops a coarse texture. Add the honey, milk and vanilla extract and combine well, until the dough comes together. Cover with plastic wrap and chill the dough in the refrigerator for 30 minutes.

2. Preheat the oven to 180°C. Line a baking tray with a silicon mat or parchment paper.

3. Roll out the chilled dough between 2 sheets of parchment paper and cut out squares measuring 6x6 cm. Transfer the squares onto the baking tray and prick using a fork or skewer. Bake them for 12–15 minutes, or until they become golden brown. Cool the crackers on a wire rack.

4. Take a graham cracker and spread an even layer of chocolate ganache on it using an offset spatula or a spoon. Place marshmallows on top of the ganache and toast them using a blowtorch. Cover with another graham cracker.

CHOCOLATE ECLAIRS WITH HAZELNUT PRALINE

I love desserts (obviously!), but if I had to pick one that I would eat at all times of the day, it would be these over-the-top eclairs! The combination of hazelnut praline with the whipped cream and chocolate is simply divine.

INGREDIENTS

For the choux pastry

1 cup water
½ cup cold butter, cubed
1 cup all-purpose flour
4 eggs

For the filling

1 cup whipping cream
½ cup hazelnut praline
(see p. 53)
1 cup dark chocolate, to dip

METHOD

1. Preheat the oven to 200°C. Line a baking tray with parchment paper.

2. To make the choux pastry, bring the water and butter to a boil in a saucepan set over medium heat. Using salted butter for the dough prevents the éclairs from cracking. Take the mixture off the heat and add all the flour at once. Mix vigorously till the dough begins to come together and forms a ball. Make sure there are no flour pockets. Immediately set the saucepan on low heat and cook the dough for another 3–5 minutes. Doing this is essential because it dries out the excess water from the dough. You'll know it is done when you see a thin layer of starch coating the bottom of the pan.

3. Take the dough off the heat and let it cool before adding the eggs. (Adding eggs to the hot dough will cook and curdle the eggs.) To cool the dough put it in a stand mixer with a paddle attachment and let it run on slow for a few minutes. If you don't have a stand mixer, keep mixing the dough with a wooden spoon to let the hot steam escape.

4. Add the eggs, one at a time, mixing well after each addition. Once you've added the eggs the choux pastry may look like its falling apart. Just keep

mixing until it comes together. Transfer the pastry to a piping bag fitted with a 1-cm round nozzle and pipe oblongs of dough on the baking tray. Dip your finger in cold water and even out the shape and smoothen the edges of the oblongs.

5. Bake the pastry for 10 minutes. Reduce the temperature to 165°C and bake for another 20 minutes until the éclairs become rich brown in colour. It is important to bake the éclairs at the temperatures mentioned. Do not open the oven door while they are baking, otherwise they will collapse. Once the éclairs are done, open the oven door just a little bit and let them cool gradually.

6. While the éclairs are cooling, whip the heavy cream on medium high speed until it forms stiff peaks. Fold in the hazelnut praline until well combined. Transfer the filling into a piping bag attached with a large star tip.

7. Slice the éclairs into half, horizontally, and dip the outside of the top half into the melted chocolate.

8. Pipe the hazelnut praline filling on the bottom half by making swirls. Cover with the top half.

PARIS BREST

Paris Brest is a dessert that was created in 1910 to celebrate the Paris–Brest bicycle race in France. Give in to temptation and go recreate this famous fancy choux pastry treat in your own kitchen!

INGREDIENTS

For the choux pastry

1 cup water
½ cup cold butter, cubed
1 cup all-purpose flour, sifted twice
4 eggs
¼ cup flaked almonds, to top

For the filling

1 cup white chocolate, chopped roughly
¾ cup fresh cream
1 cup whipped cream
1 cup fresh strawberries, cut in half

For the topping

Icing sugar, to dust

METHOD

1. Preheat the oven to 200°C. Line a baking tray with parchment paper.

2. To make the choux pastry, bring the water and butter to a boil in a saucepan set over medium heat. Take the mixture off the heat and add all flour at once. Stir vigorously until the dough begins to come together and forms a ball. Make sure there are no flour pockets. Immediately set the mixture back over low heat and cook for another 3–5 minutes. You'll know it is done when you see a thin layer of starch coating the bottom of the pan. Take the pan off the heat and let the choux cool completely. Add the eggs, one at a time, mixing well after each addition.

3. Transfer the choux pastry dough into a piping bag attached to a 1-cm round nozzle and pipe the dough into rings of around 2.5-inch diameter on the prepared baking sheet. Sprinkle the flaked almonds on top of the rings. Bake for 20 minutes, or until the choux rings have puffed up and are golden brown. Let them cool.

4. To make the filling, put the chopped chocolate in a bowl and set aside. Warm the cream in a saucepan over medium heat until just simmering and pour it over the chopped chocolate. Let it sit for 5 minutes, then stir until the mixture is smooth. Refrigerate for 30–40 minutes, until the white chocolate ganache is set. Fold it into the whipped cream, which will make the ganache light and airy.

5. Slice the choux rings horizontally into half. Pipe swirls of the lightened white chocolate ganache onto the bottom half and alternate with fresh strawberries. Cover with the top half and dust with icing sugar.

TIRAMISU MOUSSE

What's light, smooth, fluffy and feels like a coffee hug? This delicious
tiramisu mousse served with some crisp ladyfinger cookies.

INGREDIENTS

½ cup chopped white
chocolate
¼ cup fresh cream
½ cup mascarpone cheese
¾ cup whipped cream
2 shots of espresso
3–4 lady finger biscuits,
to top

METHOD

1. Put the chopped chocolate in a bowl and set aside.

2. Heat the cream in a saucepan until it begins
   to simmer. Pour the warm cream over the white
   chocolate. Let it stand for 5 minutes then stir
   until the mixture is smooth and creamy. Chill the
   ganache in the refrigerator for 1 hour, till it sets.

3. Once the ganache has cooled, fold in the
   mascarpone cheese and whipped cream and
   mix until well combined. Set ¼ cup of this white
   chocolate mousse aside. Add the espresso shots
   to the rest of the mousse and mix well.

4. Spoon the espresso mousse into the serving dish
   or glasses and top it with a dollop of the white
   chocolate mousse.

5. Chill the mousse in the refrigerator for 30 minutes.
   Garnish with ladyfinger biscuits before serving.

INDEX

ACKNOWLEDGEMENTS

When I started working on my second book, I knew the process of working on 100 recipes, testing and retesting them and then styling and shooting them all would not be a cakewalk. But I was confident I would be able to pull it off, given the unconditional support of some very special people. I must thank:

Firstly, the readers of my blog, my Instagram fam and my YouTube subscribers for being my virtual family, for encouraging me and loving me. It's only because of you that I've become the author of two books!

My family, especially Mummy, Papa and Shubhra, for never letting me doubt my decisions and being my biggest cheerleaders. To know you've got my back and that everything will be fine as long as I'm with you is the best feeling ever.

Navrup and Arushi for working tirelessly on this book with me and helping me test and retest the recipes. This book is yours as much as it is mine! Thank you for making the process of working on this book so much fun.

Hridey, for helping me with the edits and proofreading – the part I like the least. But you made it seamless and so smooth! I couldn't have done it without you.

Priyanshi, Archita, Rajat and Ria for holding fort and making sure everything else was taken care of. Thank you for always being there for when I needed you through the process of creating this book. I truly have the most incredible team!

Kritika, Saif and Tanya for telling me I could do it every time I thought it was too tough and for helping me make the tough decisions. You're my best friends, my favourite critics and my very own board of advisors.

Shweta, Trisha, Gunjan, Sahiba, Amrita, Varun, Lyimee, Shreya, Rukmini, Ankrish, Himansh and Shruti for being my constant source of support. I know I can count on you!

Sana Jaisingh, for your impeccable sartorial choices, and styling me for the photoshoot.

My publisher, Diya. Shreya, for believing in me and giving me this opportunity. Bushra, for always being a call away and patiently dealing with the most stressed-out author ever! Bonita, for understanding my sensibilities like no other. Shatarupa, Isha, Sagiri, Amit and everyone at HarperCollins who has worked on and made this book possible.

ABOUT THE AUTHOR

Shivesh Bhatia has a following of over 5 million across social media platforms and has been sharing recipes on his blog, Bake With Shivesh, for over ten years now. In 2023, he was named in the Forbes 30 Under 30 (Asia - Media, Marketing and Advertising) list, and was ranked among India's Top 100 Digital Stars by Forbes. He received the Inspiring Personality In Culinary Excellence award at the Global Excellence Awards, 2024.

He is the author of *Bake with Shivesh*, *Eggless Baking with Shivesh* and has a baking book for children: *A Cookbook for Special Days, Special People.*